Executive Information
Systems and Decision Support

UNICOM Applied Information Technology

Each book in the series is based upon papers given at a seminar organized by UNICOM Seminars Ltd. The reports cover subjects at the forefront of information technology, and the contributors are all authorities in the subject on which they are invited to write, either as researchers or as practitioners.

Executive Information Systems and Decision Support

UNICOM
APPLIED INFORMATION TECHNOLOGY 15

Edited by **Clive Holtham**

City University Business School, London

CHAPMAN & HALL

London · Glasgow · New York · Tokyo · Melbourne · Madras

Published by Chapman & Hall, 2-6 Boundary Row, London SE1 8HN, UK

Chapman & Hall, 2-6 Boundary Row, London SE1 8HN, UK

Blackie Academic & Professional, Wester Cleddens Road, Bishopbriggs, Glasgow G64 2NZ, UK

Chapman & Hall GmbH, Pappelallee 3, 69469 Weinheim, Germany

Chapman & Hall Inc., One Penn Plaza, 41st Floor, New York, NY10119, USA

Chapman & Hall Japan, Thomson Publishing Japan, Hirakawacho Nemoto Building, 6F, 1-7-11 Hirakawa-cho, Chiyoda-ku, Tokyo 102, Japan

Chapman & Hall Australia, Thomas Nelson Australia, 102 Dodds Street, South Melbourne, Victoria 3205, Australia

Chapman & Hall India, R. Seshadri, 32 Second Main Road, CIT East, Madras 600 035, India

First edition 1992

© 1992 UNICOM and contributors

Printed in Great Britain by Ipswich Book Company, Ipswich, Suffolk

ISBN 0 412 44770 3   0 442 31570 8 (USA)

The publisher makes no representation, express or implied, with regard to the accuracy of the information contained in this book and cannot accept any legal responsibility or liability for any errors or omissions that may be made.

A catalogue record for this book is available from the British Library

Library of Congress Cataloging-in-publication data available

Contents

CONTRIBUTORS

C. W. Holtham
City University Business School
Frobisher Crescent
Barbican Centre
London
EC2Y 8HB

K. Eason
Dept of Human Sciences
Loughborough University of
   Technology
Loughborough
Leics
LE11 3TU

Jerry Kanter
Brabson College
Wellesley
Massachusetts
USA

Robin Matthews
Kingston Business School
Kingston Polytechnic
Kingston Hill Centre
Kingston upon Thames
KT2 7LB

C. Eden
University of Strathclyde
Dept of Management Science
Livingston Tower
26 Richmond Street
Glasgow
Scotland G1 1XH

Frances Ackermann
University of Strathclyde
Dept of Management Science
Livingston Tower
26 Richmond Street
Glasgow
Scotland G1 1XH

Martin Callaghan
Mindworks
London Underground Ltd
55 Broadway
London
SW1H 0BD

A. Popovich
British Airways
Comet House
S6 BA
P.O. Box 10
Heathrow Airport
Middlesex
TW6 2JA

D. Stone
BT Plc
St Alphage House
2 Fore Street
London
EC2Y 5XA

Nigel Tout
ICL
Hedsor House
Hedsor Park
Taplow
Nr. Maidenhead
Berks
SL6 0HY

Ciaran Murphy
University College
Cork
Ireland

John D. Little
Sloane School of Management
Massachussetts Institute of Technology
Cambridge
Massachusetts
USA

L. D. Phillips
London School of Economics
Haughton Street
London
WC2A 2AE

Simon French
The University of Leeds
School of Computer Studies
Leeds
LS2 9JT

Albert A. Angehrn
INSEAD
European Institute of Business
    Administration
Bd de Constance
F – 77305 Fontainebleau
France

Raul Espejo
Operations and Information
    Management Division
Aston University
Aston Triangle
Birmingham
B4 7ET

John D. Schmitz
Information Resources
200 Fifth Ave
Waltham
Massachusetts 02154
USA

Gordon D. Armstrong
Ocean Spray Cranberries
1 Ocean Spray Drive
Lakeville-Middleboro
Massachusetts
USA

Tore Gannholm
Consultant
Stiltjevägen 28
S-132 31 Saltsjö-Boo
Sweden

Introduction

Clive Holtham
City University Business School

The subject area of Executive Information and Decision Support Systems is one that potentially spans a broad range of academic disciplines and vendor interests. Much of the existing literature tends to focus on specific parts of the subject areas. This book deliberately sets out with a broad span in mind, with a further emphasis on drawing together experiences and case studies from several different countries.

It is aimed at practitioners in these areas who seek a broader and deeper understanding, and to students on MBA, business studies, business information technology and management science courses who need to have an overview of the subject area which is rooted in both the reality of case studies as well as the influence of more research-oriented work. Each group of specialist readers will have available to them detailed literature in their specialism. This book aims to complement, exemplify and in some cases summarize the more detailed literatures.

Much of the existing literature tends to concentrate on either academic-oriented or practitioner-oriented elements. This book covers both types of orientation. It therefore runs the risk that some chapters may be too 'academic' for some practitioners and vice versa.

In reality, the boundary between the two orientations is highly blurred. Virtually all the academics writing in this volume also have extensive current consultancy interests centring around the areas covered in their chapter. Several have created commercial products out of their researches. Equally, practitioners have often contributed more general concepts or frameworks.

The overall structure of this book is to present first a series of more conceptual papers in each of four sections, covering basic principles, executive information systems, group decision support systems and multi-criteria decision making. These are followed by a number of case studies of individual organizations.

PRINCIPLES

It is appropriate that the book opens with a paper by Ken Eason of the HUSAT (Human Sciences and Advanced Technology) Research Centre at Loughborough University of Technology. HUSAT has a wealth of research-based expertise in the human aspects of systems generally, and of computer systems in particular. He is a strong advocate of socio-technical design in which the interdependence of organizational design is explicitly recognized in the systems design process. He presents a helpful framework for addressing management use of computers, showing the triangular interaction between organizational environment, functionality and method of operation. His conclusion serves as an apt introduction to the remaining chapters, and a warning that the development of systems to provide executives with information is far from straightforward:

'An analysis of the history of computer-based systems for managers reveals many failures. The major difficulty is that the management environment is hostile to such systems; the information needs are complex and variable and the users have little time or inclination to learn or adapt.'

The second chapter is by Jerry Kanter of Babson College. Before moving into the academic world, Jerry had spent much of his career involved in consultancy with top managers, and he draws on this experience in outlining a personal view of why and how chief executives need to develop what he describes as 'information literacy'. He is well aware of the difficulties involved in this task, but makes a variety of practical suggestions on how to overcome these difficulties.

EXECUTIVE INFORMATION SYSTEMS

Executive Information Systems (EIS) only came into existence in the second half of the 1980s, at least in the sense of a definable category of software.

This section is introduced by Robin Matthews of the Kingston Business School, who first sets out a framework for understanding the role of information and executive information systems. This is followed by a report of the findings of three separate surveys carried out on UK companies between 1987 and 1990, reviewing amongst other matters the actual use of EIS software packages. Several conclusions followed, including the risks of dependence on a particular management style which 'leaves an enormous gap in the information structure'. Events in several high-profile UK-based businesses since Matthews completed his paper have only served to underline his analysis that internal information systems appear not to be always providing reliable and accurate historic or planning information, in particular to non-executive directors and others in stewardship roles.

The other paper in this section is by Clive Holtham of the City University Business School, who reviews some of the literature which describes managerial roles, and then compares these roles to the functions that have to date been conventionally addressed by EIS software. There is a gap between the two, and Holtham suggests this gap can be filled on the one hand by a 'next-generation' EIS that will take on board a much greater orientation towards 'soft' data, as well as use of multi-media. He also describes a research project with company directors, one output from which is software aimed at increasing directors' awareness of the contribution of IT to them personally.

GROUP DECISION SUPPORT SYSTEMS

Most of the thrust of the development of decision support systems in the 1970s was with problems that could be addressed by assuming that decisions were taken by one person or the equivalent. During the 1980s a number of approaches have been developed which are preoccupied with the more realistic yet rather more problematic decision-making unit, namely the group.

The approaches to Group Decision Support Systems (GDSS) in the UK has tended to emphasize the inter-personal and 'softer' aspects of decision-making, while at least some of the North American approaches are rather more formalistic. Two of the UK's leading groups of academics in this area outline their respective approaches in this section.

Lawrence Phillips of the Decision Analysis Unit at the London School of Economics describes the use of the decision conferencing, with particular reference to the use of the unit's HIVIEW software and, using an illustration, a typical business strategy problem. Phillips highlights seven important issues which can be identified as common to many senior managers, and his succinct conclusion after discussing these issues is that 'there is a need to improve decision taking in organizations', but that this need is far from well recognized.

From the Strategic Decision Support Research Unit at the University of Strathclyde Business School, Colin Eden and Fran Ackermann describe the principles of strategy development as well as their methodology known as Strategic Options Development and Analysis (SODA) and the related software COPE. These 'allow a group to "play with" their ideas about strategy through the real-time interaction with graphical computer representations and analyses of their data'. The authors argue that this type of system can be used in two ways as an EIS; first by requiring that major decisions are made by direct reference to the model, and second because it becomes the basis for review of all subordinate staff.

SUPPORTING MULTI-CRITERIA DECISIONS

Many decisions in business and the public sector are not based on single criteria, indeed almost all the most significant strategic decisions involve multiple-criteria. Managerial readers of French's paper should not be deterred by the elegant mathematics it uses to support its arguments. This paper deals with the important practical problem of sensitivity analysis, and uses an example from flood-plain management to illustrate use of sensitivity analysis. In the flood-plain example, the option that was top ranked by simple additive ranking methods is shown to be 'far from robust to small changes in judgemental inputs'. French also outlines an intriguing development under way which involves using a PC with decision-analytic software as a front-end, the solution of individual problems being farmed out to individual transputers. This could enable real-world-sized problems to be addressed in near-real time.

Albert Angehrn is one of Europe's leading young researchers in the field of decision support systems. He has already been awarded by the Institute of Management Sciences (Distinguished Contribution Award at the First International Competition for Outstanding Decision Support Applications and Achievements) and by Apple Computers France (Apple Trophy 1990 for the best system-enhancing personal productivity developed in 1990). He is involved in the integration of management science and artificial intelligence approaches into computer-supported decision making, yet his paper on multi-criteria decision places a welcome emphasis on the humanization of decision support. He urges the need to move from an over-simplistic model of 'objective reality' towards models which accept that for many problems there are in practice a variety of different 'subjective realities'. To assist in this, Angehrn has developed a visually-oriented tool – Triple C. This is aimed at facilitating incremental problem structuring, individual exploration of the space of alternatives, and then easy communication of the results. An example from a recruitment task is used to illustrate Triple C in action.

CASE STUDIES

One of the most perceptive thinkers in management science has been Stafford Beer, and one of Beer's close associates, Raul Espejo of the Aston Business School, has developed software (Cyberfilter) that embodies many of the principles of management cybernetics propounded by Beer. Espejo identifies a major gulf between the two worlds of data processing and of management reporting, and argues that a tool such as Cyberfilter is essential to provide a soundly-based method of filtering and presenting data. He recognizes, however, that this particular approach challenges many widely-held preconceptions of managers, but that as long as the preconceptions are held they will limit managers' real ability to control their organizations.

The London Underground may be the subject of a variety of criticism, but in order to improve its performance has set up a variety of initiatives to improve managerial and organizational performance. Martin Callaghan of Mindworks has been working at London Underground to promote Total Quality Management (TQM), specifically with reference to EIS and DSS. He illustrates how relatively straightforward executive information systems can be used to focus the organization on specific goals. However, his overall argument is that to be really successful such systems must be embedded in an appropriate managerial philosophy, such as that of TQM.

One of the UK's first recognized success stories in the development of EIS has been British Airways, with its AIMS system now having developed beyond a relatively small number of top executive users to become a tool of senior managers also. Aleks Popovich, as manager of the MERLIN EIS project within British Airways, gives a useful historical analysis of the development and use of AIMS, particularly in the context of the corporate development of the company. He then goes on to describe the new MERLIN system. This is being developed in-house on a Windows platform, but Popovich warns that this approach can only be sustained where there is 'considerable confidence in the IT function's technical capabilities'.

David Stone of British Telecom was involved in the implementation of no less than four EIS systems in an eighteen-month period, and is therefore well placed to discuss the design features and architectures that were relevant to the company. He argues strongly for the 'top-down' approach to EIS design, well aware that this approach is likely to attract criticism from traditional systems departments. His chapter gives a useful insight into the reality of EIS project management in a large business.

Following on from the earlier chapters on GDSS, Nigel Tout of ICL describes how his company has used decision conferencing for UK clients to plan prioritization of their IT investment. This has often taken place as part of a broader executive education programme. He draws on a specific case study from a major service organization, and gives some detailed illustrations of the kinds of trade-offs involved, and emphasizes the significance of a facilitator in this type of process.

Ciaran Murphy, of University College, Cork, uses a case study of Southern Isle Financial Services to develop some fundamental points in relation to the DSS framework originally developed by Gorry and Scott Morton.

The Ocean Spray Cranberries case study has been written jointly by a member of its own staff (Gordon D. Armstrong), an employee of the vendor of the expert systems software used – CoverStory from Information Resources (John D. Schmitz), and the academic from MIT who has developed many of the underlying principles in the software (John D.C.

Little). The case is an excellent example of how relevant information can be filtered from the vast quantities of data now readily available, in the USA at least, from very large marketing databases using data from scanner-equipped stores. The CoverStory system can ultimately produce reports with graphs, tables and conclusions in desktop-publishing format. But the authors are quick to point out that this is still a decision-support system, not a decision-making system.

In conclusion, this book emerged from a Unicom seminar of the same title, and I would particularly like to thank the staff of Unicom Ltd for their diligence during the editing of this book, in particular Mrs Dhira Mitra who was responsible for much of the administrative aspect of the editing.

Part One

Principles

1 Organizational issues in the use of decision support systems

K. Eason
HUSAT Research Institute, Loughborough University of Technology

1.1 THE PROBLEM

There have been many attempts to develop computer-based information systems to serve management over the past thirty years. The management environment is dedicated to information processing and computer systems should be of considerable benefit to managers. Attempts in the 1960s to create management information systems (MISs) were not successful, leading Ackoff (1967) to christen them 'management mis-information systems'. The next generation of systems were decision-support systems (DSSs) and made more attempt than MISs to understand the decision-making character of the manager's task. There have been successes but the rate of success is still not high. In the twenty organizations studied as part of a Department of Trade and Industry investigation (Pye et al. 1986), for example, decision-support applications achieved a 37% success rate compared with 60% for text processing applications. The main problem is that the manager is a very difficult user to serve. It is the contention of this paper that executive information systems (EISs) will succeed to the extent that they can accurately support the needs of management users. To support this contention the paper will first explore the characteristics of the management task and environment which have been causing difficulty. Thereafter the intention is to explore the properties that EISs will have to include in order to be successful and the process necessary for successful development and implementation.

1.2 MANAGERIAL RESPONSES TO COMPUTER AIDS

As a result of studying 82 managers who used between them sixteen decision support systems, Eason (1981) developed the framework, shown in Figure 1.1, to account for managerial responses to these systems. The dominant responses were disuse, distant use or partial use. In many cases the majority of the intended users did not use the system. In some cases the managers made use of the systems but, rather than direct 'hands-on' interaction via a terminal or personal computer, they used the system via an intermediary: an information officer, secretary etc. Where managers did make direct use of a system, they restricted themselves to partial use of the facilities available. In many instances this was quite dramatic; in one case a manager limited his use to regular checks of the company's latest share price. None of these responses can be said to be making good use of system potential.

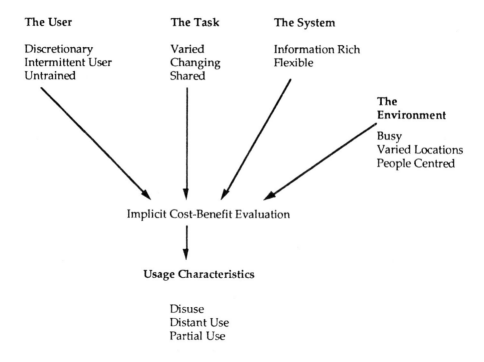

The User

Discretionary
Intermittent User
Untrained

The Task

Varied
Changing
Shared

The System

Information Rich
Flexible

The Environment

Busy
Varied Locations
People Centred

Implicit Cost-Benefit Evaluation

Usage Characteristics

Disuse
Distant Use
Partial Use

Fig. 1.1 Managerial responses to computer systems (after Eason [1981]).

Why do manager's respond in this way? It is first important to recognize that managers are intermittent, discretionary users, i.e. they only use systems occasionally having many other activities to perform and they have choice over whether and when they use it. The more senior they are the less likely are they to accept any dictates that they should use a system. These characteristics have two consequences. First, intermittent use means they tend not to remember from one occasion to the next how to operate the system. Second, being discretionary means they must see some value in using the system, not only the system as a whole but each facility within it. The most important element in this explanatory framework, therefore, is the implicit cost-benefit evaluation the manager makes before and during the use of the system. This is not to say that the manager carefully weighs up the value of each transaction; it is to say there must be a perceived value to each transaction and that, during the transaction, there will be checks on the effort needed to achieve this value and if progress is hard or slow or success unlikely, the exercise will be aborted.

Many other users show similar characteristics but managers seem particularly intolerant. In part this is because they tend to be very busy with an unending array of problems to confront and the need to continuously review priorities for the use of their time. The popularity of time-management courses is testament to this pressure. A related issue is that the average manager spends very little time alone in his/her office and in a position to make use of the average system which is presented through a visual display unit in the manager's office. A study of American managers by Mintzberg (1973) found they spent only 22% of their time in desk work (and nearly 70% of time in meetings). A UK study by Wainwright and Francis (1984) found 22% devoted to desk work (and 53% to meetings). The environment is therefore essentially people-centred and provides little time for long sessions of computer interaction.

All of these characteristics would be of little significance if the manager only needed to use a limited range of facilities to meet the task needs. A simpler system can be mastered by an intelligent person even in the difficult setting described above. However, management is about the new, the unexpected, the exceptional, and this means each information processing task may need a different set of data and a different set of facilities to process them. The changeable nature of the task means the system to serve the manager has to have a rich store of information and a flexible way of processing this information. The evidence from the survey showed that as the system became sufficiently powerful and flexible to meet the manager's needs so it tended to become too complex for the manager to use with the limited time that was available. It is also very unlikely that the manager will come equipped with the range of information-technology knowledge and skills necessary to make immediate use of the system. The designer is therefore on the horns of a dilemma. A simple system which a manager would find easy to use would probably be of little value for most of the tasks to be undertaken. A system sufficiently complex to meet the array of task needs may be too difficult for the manager to master. Small wonder the result has so often been disuse or partial use. The distant use strategy is of particular interest because in theory it enables the manager to get the value from the system whilst passing the load of understanding the operational detail to somebody else. The question then is whether this form of 'interaction' can give the manager the same level of support for the task as direct interaction.

1.3   REQUIREMENTS FOR AN EXECUTIVE INFORMATION SYSTEM

The definition of an Executive Information System will no doubt concentrate upon the specific functionality needed to support particular management tasks, whether it be financial planning, performance monitoring, exception reporting, or 'what happens if?' modelling etc. However, the analysis of the managerial environment identifies a range of additional requirements that have to be met if the manager is to find this functionality directly accessible. These requirements are listed in Figure 1.2 under three headings.

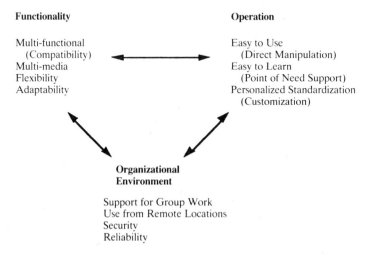

Fig. 1.2   A manager's requirements from an Executive Information System.

1.3.1 Functionality

In addition to the specific task functionality we can add three further requirements. First, any system will need to be multi-functional if it is to meet the array of managerial requirements. The manager will need access to a variety of applications and, if one system is difficult to use, to have to use a number of incompatible systems for different systems will be impossible. Integrated, compatible systems which, for example, give local facilities personal to the user and access to the company databases, will be necessary to serve the managerial environment. The system will need to offer multi-media output facilities (words, numbers, graphics, speech etc.) so that the most appropriate presentation media can be used for each task and the system needs to offer flexibility so that the manager can find the most relevant service from the array available. A related issue is that the manager's needs and knowledge will change and grow and the system must grow and adapt in the facilities it offers if it is to remain a valuable resource to the manager.

1.3.2 Operation

It is a necessary but not sufficient condition for use for the system to have perceived benefit in its functionality. It also needs to be possible for managers to use the system directly despite the difficult environment in which they work. Use of Decision Support Systems HUSAT Research Institute, Department of Human Sciences, Loughborough University of Technology, Leics. LE11 3TU.

1.3.3 Organizational environment

The organizational environment of the manager produces a further set of requirements. Managers tend to work through meetings with subordinates, colleagues, customers etc. and a useful system is one that supports the work of people who share a common task. Similarly there is little point in making the manager's office the only place in which the system can be used if the manager is away most of the time. The development of portable terminals and mobile systems may have an important role to play in future systems, enabling managers to interact with databases and colleagues whilst away from the office. Two related issues which may be stringent requirements for managers are reliability and security. If information is important, managers who commit themselves to depending on systems will need assurances that nothing disastrous can happen if the system crashes. Similarly they will need assurances that information with significant implications can be securely held, protected from both outside 'hackers' and (in all probability) unauthorized colleagues and subordinates.

1.4   ORGANIZATIONAL ISSUES IN THE IMPLEMENTATION OF SYSTEMS

The evidence from many implementations shows quite clearly that success is heavily dependent upon the way the system is implemented and the organizational support it receives when in place. Figure 1.3 lists the major factors that have been found to be important.

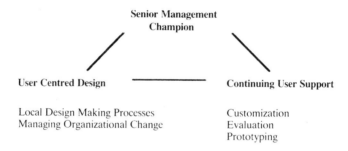

Senior Management Champion

User Centred Design   **Continuing User Support**

Local Design Making Processes   Customization
Managing Organizational Change   Evaluation
                                   Prototyping

Fig. 1.3   Organisational issues in the implementation of computer-based systems to support managers.

The most important factor is that implementation should be user centred. This does not mean the users dominate proceedings because they may have little understanding of what is possible or desirable. Rather it means that developers must endeavour to work with users throughout the process to help users express their requirements and become committed to the solutions that are offered (Eason 1988). Part of this process will be concerned with the analysis of local decision-making processes in order that the system supports real rather than imagined managerial tasks. There have been many cases where the designers have become fascinated by the management task and have designed very sophisticated ways of dealing with it only to find they have moved so far away from the user's 'model' of the task that the system is useless to them. In one instance we studied a very sophisticated model of a life assurance company that had been built to support long-term policy making. It was only after it had been simplified to a level managers could understand that it became useful in the organization. It is often the case that utilization of a system requires organizational change, may be new roles and responsibilities for staff, may be shared working from different locations by new groups of people, etc. The design and development of these new ways of working may be as important as the design of the technical system.

When it is implemented, as discussed above, the system will almost certainly need a very active support officer to encourage and support learning and use. The support will also need to provide customization of interfaces and the development of local applications to serve the unique requirements of specific users. Most successful systems also show an evolutionary pattern of development, beginning with relatively few facilities and developing more as and when the user population identifies the need for them and can cope with their usage. It might well be that the original system has the capability to offer a wide variety of facilities. However, in order to avoid overwhelming the user it may be best to follow a policy of progressive disclosure, making facilities available as and when users are ready. An important element of evolutionary development is the prototyping of new services in order that users can make informed judgements about what they want and the form in which they want it. A final consideration, as McCosh (1984) noted in his analysis of fifteen decision-support systems, is that the system will need the continual support of a senior management champion. McCosh noted that in a number of instances systems were stopped by management at a level above the users of the system. These senior managers may have concluded that there was heavy investment for a little return, may have been worried by use of high technology in a way they did not understand or may simply have other priorities for expenditure. Whatever the reason, they were in a position to take this action regardless of the success of the system. The enduring success of any system is always dependent upon senior committed supporters who can promote its cause at the highest levels.

1.5 CONCLUSIONS

It is conventional to argue that systems to support managers are cost-effective because they will enable managers to make more effective decisions. Such approaches are necessary but not sufficient to the successful implementation of systems. An analysis of the history of computer-based systems for managers reveals many failures. The major difficulty is that the management environment is hostile to such systems; the information needs are complex and variable and the users have little time or inclination to learn or adapt. In such circumstances it is the character of the system that must adapt by being easy to use and easy to learn and it is the system development process that must mould itself for user and organizational characteristics.

Similarly very to meet the array of managerial requirements. The manager will need access to a variety of applications and, if one system is difficult to use, to have to use a number of incompatible systems for different systems will be impossible. Integrated, compatible systems which, for example, give local facilities.

REFERENCES

Ackoff, R. L. (1967) Management misinformation systems, *Management Science*, 14, 4.

Eason, K. D. (1981) Manager-computer interaction: a study of a task-tool relationship, Doctoral Thesis, Loughborough University of Technology.

Eason, K. D. (1988) *Information Technology and Organizational Change*, London, Taylor Francis.

McCosh, A. M. (1984) Factors common to the successful implementation of 12 decision support systems and how they differ from 3 failures, *Systems, Objectives, Solutions*, 4, 17-28.

Mintzberg, H. (1973) *The Nature of Managerial Work*, New York, Harper & Row.

Wainwright, J. and Francis, A. (1984) *Office Automation, Organisation and the Nature of Work*, Aldershot, Gower.

2 Information literacy for the CEO

J. Kanter
Babson College, Wellesley, MA

2.1 INTRODUCTION

A survey conducted by Kepner-Tregoe of 800 Chief Executive Officers and Chief Operating Officers of Fortune 500 Companies indicated that 70% of the executives do not have a terminal or personal computer in their office (Kepner-Tregoe 1986). *Personal Computing* magazine received 488 replies from CEOs of the 500 top US corporations(Honan 1986). Their survey showed that 87% of the CEOs do notuse a personal computer in their office. The author's experience supports these statistics and suggests that most ofthose who do not have PCs in the office use them infrequently,if at all.

'Computer literacy' is a popular term, but a vague one at best. Most often it refers to a familiarity with the use of personal computers including both hardware and software operation. So, by this definition, most CEOs and Chief Operating Officers are probably 'computer illiterate'. But have we properly defined 'literacy' from their perspective? My purpose is to define computer literacy for the CEO, to discuss why it is important, and to develop a program for attaining it.

A reasonable definition of the term is essential, but I would prefer to shift the emphasis from the computer literacy to 'information literacy'. Computer literacy suggests that one must be able to operate a computer with the requisite keyboard skills and software and hardware knowledge. By information literacy I mean an understanding of the general concepts of information processing. How do computer systems support and/or shape a person's job function? What are the trade-offs between investments and benefits, time expended and time saved?

What are the feasible application areas? The concentration here is on 'why' and 'what', not on 'how'. Rapid advances in technology have changed the balance of those trade-offs, but nonetheless they are still present. My point is that computer literacy is not the main issue: information literacy is.

Most CEOs and senior managers, now in their late forties or fifties, rarely discussed information systems during their college years. What they learned has been acquired on the job or through a variety of continuing education programs. Recently, however, prominent institutions like Carnegie Mellon and the Harvard Business School have made the purchase of a personal computer a requirement similar to the payment of tuition, room and board. And although some question the logic and rationale for this decision, few customers (students) or faculty have the information literacy necessary to challenge the decision.

2.2   TWO INFORMATION SYSTEM ROLES FOR THE CEO

There are two roles regarding information systems that the CEO must be aware of. The first is as a direct user; that is, employing a terminal or PC in his office to directly access information inside or outside the company, to send electronic messages, maintain his calendar, or do spreadsheet-like calculations for analysis or decision support. The second role is that of an overseer of the use of information systems in the functions of the company for which he or she has responsibility. I have come to the conclusion that we have allowed our preoccupation with the direct-user role to warp our perspective on the much more important overseer role.

In my opinion, it is strictly management style or personal preference that dictates whether a senior manager will be comfortable using a PC. There are left-brain managers (intuitive), and I think there always will be. It is also true that there are still many business events that cannot be neatly plugged into the aseptic cells of a spreadsheet. I have a feeling that, despite the progressively earlier introduction of PCs into the educational process, the right-brained will still be tomorrow's CEOs and senior managers.

John Deardon of the Harvard Business School has always taken the traditional position that the computer will not have a major impact on the basic management process. He wrote in 1966 that senior managers do not need real-time data to manage unless they are watching things like day-to-day production activity, which should properly be a delegated responsibility (Deardon 1966). He added in 1972 that 'a company that pursues an MIS [Management Information System] embarks on a wild-goose chase, a search for a will-o'-the-wisp' (Deardon 1972). Finally, in 1983 he stated that a computer would not have any important impact on the way a manager manages (Deardon 1983). I have disagreed with Dr Deardon's conservative positions over the years, but experience is giving credence to his views. He takes an extreme position, but makes some telling points. I think we should particularly heed his advice not to do those things that should be delegated. The danger of inappropriate use could be accentuated by the man datory status of PCs by business schools.

However, use of the computer can aid information literacy. Using a personal computer enables the CEO, by doing and making mistakes, to learn that there is something more to information systems than pressing buttons; however, it is not an end in itself. Another part of computer literacy, what I could call a technical awareness, is knowledge of the technological enablers that are changing the cost/benefit trade-offs. Since a PC is a microcosm of a larger computer system, shared concepts like database, operating systems, telecommunications and software languages can be better understood by hands-on experience.

However, despite the above, in the current state of affairs I see the PC getting in the way of the CEO. The PC can both shape and support a senior manager's job; that creates a dilemma. The nature of the CEO job makes it unlikely that a PC can shape the job (i.e. change the things done or the ways in which they are done) and the state-of-the-art in 'user-friendliness' does not make it an easy-to-use support tool. The PC must become much more 'CEO-literate' before it becomes commonplace in CEO offices. It must become like the other forms of electronics that are transparent to the user − the telephone in our office, the control system in our car, or the security system in our home.

I have stressed that, although it may be a factor to consider, computer literacy is not the key issue for the CEO. The major issue is information literacy, on which we now focus. I shall first discuss what constitutes information literacy, and then how that literacy could be attained.

2.3   INFORMATION LITERACY : THE CONTENT

As stated, what I think important to the CEO is information literacy. The CEO must recognise that information is an asset and a strategic commodity to a company. CEOs must also realize the cost and energy that must be expended to capture, store, maintain, and communicate that information throughout the organisation. The CEO must have an 'information perspective', to know when an information demand should be handled within minutes and when it's going to take years (it is essential to be able to distinguish the trivial from the blockbuster). CEOs must know their part in being able to use information strategically. And they must set priorities, place some sort of value on the information requested and specify what he or the corporate office really needs.

By this description, it becomes apparent that CEO information illiteracy is far less than the 70% suggested by the Kepner-Tregoe study or the 87% indicated in the *Personal Computing* survey. I believe CEOs have a general awareness that the technology not only presents opportunities within their organisations, but also has reached a stage where information can provide a competitive edge. The literature is replete with examples, the most frequently mentioned being American Airlines, American Hospital Supply, and McKesson Corp. However, I believe CEOs must ensure that their organization makes the most advantageous use of information. To gain the needed perspective, which to me is tantamount to information literacy, the CEO must have an understanding in several areas.

2.3.1 Databases, data and information

Dr Efrem Mallach, who conducts a two-day workshop on information literacy, builds on the premise that:
  'People simply do not know how to use data well. They do not fully understand where it comes from, how it is updated, how it is manipulated. They do not know how accurate it is in a given situation, or what factors affect its accuracy. They do not understand data security or the dangers of not having it'(Mallach 1986).
  Databases remain the cornerstone of IS. The major activities of a company revolve around a set of data files, which normally include customers, products, inventory, financial accounts and personnel. In addition, there are specialized data files such as competitive product and key economic indicators whose source is often outside the company. Applications revolve around building and compiling data (raw material) and processing that data into information (finished goods). Managers need a basic understanding of how data is captured and organized so that it can be available for management reports as well as for the daily transactions of the enterprise.

2.3.2 Telecommunications: centralization versus decentralization

The two principal functions of information systems are processing information and then communicating it. The communications world is changing faster than the processing world and the changes in the next five years will be even more crucial. Voice and data will be transmitted over the same digital circuit, allowing huge cost savings for those who can take advantage of this new technology. While the basis of the decisions are technical ones, managers need a perspective on the subject. Historically, the costs of connecting systems in disparate locations have influenced whether one designs a centralized or a decentralized information systems operation. The substitution of optical fibre for copper wire will change these cost trade-offs and allow innovative new looks at the way humans and computers communicate.

2.3.3 Transfer of information management to end-users

The proper management of this shift is one of the most signifi cant issues facing companies. The advent of personal computing and 'easier to use' languages has acted as the catalyst to this all-pervasive trend. Corporate IS must be able to control but not manage the company's information system resource. Controlling implies establishing the common conduits (database, telecommunications and overall data architecture) and standards to provide for data integration when it is necessary. Managing information is determining what to do with the data, what applications are needed and, more and more, these activities are moving under the purview of line management.

2.3.4 Prioritization of applications system development

One of the most important tasks relating to Information Systems is the determination of what application system should be implemented next. The common ailment of IS operations these days is application backlog, and with the emergence of Information Systems as strategic weapons, the priority process becomes all the more significant.

The CEO should have an understanding of the elements to be con sidered in the company prioritization process and indeed should lend his direction in placing weight on the various elements. For example, common prioritization criteria are return on investment, intangible benefits and impact, fit with corporate business direction, and technical and business risk. It is usually true that those developments with higher risk also promise the higher return. Establishing the company propensity for risk is an important senior management prerogative. A discussion and understanding of this subject is key to building information literacy.

2.3.5 The enabling technologies

Specific technologies will have significant impact on business in the next five to ten years. Two such technologies are voice recognition systems and artificial intelligence. Voice recognition offers an exciting but natural way to provide input as well as instructions to information systems; it could remove the typing requirement that has long discouraged executives and professionals from becoming direct users. Artificial intelligence can provide a natural language interface to information systems that can accommodate individual language styles; and Expert Systems, a major component of artificial intelligence, can 'clone' (via computer software) the logic of professionals in dealing with and resolving complex problems. Expert Systems are a follow-on stage to Decision Support Systems used today in many corporations. These are just two of the enabling technologies that should be watched and understood.

2.3.6 Information system policies

Information policies are becoming very important as guidelines to controlling and directing the use of technology within an organisation. Compatibility and integration are essential objectives of a company-wide information system, but without meaningful policies those objectives will never be reached.

The CEO should be aware of and involved in the policies of IS that govern elements like data and security standards, acquisition of resources (including personal computers), communications protocols, roles of privacy and ethics, responsibilities of end-user departments versus the IS group, and other policies that are significant to the effective operation of IS within the company. Also important are policies concerned with the operation of steering committees or user groups that give valuable direction to IS activities. In my opinion, an understanding of existing and needed policies and their relevance to IS functions is a basic part of information literacy.

2.4   INFORMATION LITERACY: THE PROCESS

We have discussed the content of information literacy, that is, 'what' constitutes it. The six areas described represent the basic underpinnings of CEO literacy. We now turn to the process of 'how' that literacy is developed. The steps to be described should not be construed as the total prescription for literacy. They can be viewed instead as a starter set, a motivator for a continued awareness and involvement in information system matters.

An important benefit of this process is that this top-down approach can set the stage for an education strategy for other senior managers within the organization. It is a corporate fact of life in companies that the style and operational mode of the CEO is emulated by his subordinates. By following the steps described, the CEO can acquire information literacy, and the other managers can benefit as well.

2.4.1 Assess the CEO's management style

This assessment is an important first step since business managers operate in a variety of ways.

Henry Mintzberg, a well-known pragmatic management researcher, challenges the common view of managers as reflective, regulated, rational, and scientific professionals. Rather, he emphatically describes what management is really all about:

'The facts show the manager works at a relentless pace. His activities are characterised by brevity, variety and discontinuity. He is strongly oriented to action and dislikes reflective activities' (Mintzberg 1975).

Mintzberg says if there is a single characteristic in the practice of management it is that:

'The pressures of his job drive the manager to be superficial in his actions — to overload himself with work, encourage interruptions, respond quickly to every stimulus, seek the tangible and avoid the abstract, make decisions in small increments and do everything abruptly.'

John Rockart describes the antithesis of the Mintzberg model in relating the work style of Ben Heineman, then President and CEO of Northwest Industries.

'Northwest's Executive Information System with its extensive and continually growing database is now used by almost all managers and executives at corporate headquarters to perform their monitoring and analytic functions. But the driving force behind the system and its most significant user remains Heineman. Working with the system is an everyday thing for him, a natural part of his job. With his special knowledge of the business and with his newly acquired ability to write his own programs, Heineman sees great value in working at a terminal himself rather than handing all assignments to staff personnel.

'"There is a huge advantage to the CEO to get his hands dirty in the data," he says, "because the answers to many significant questions are found in the detail. The system provides me with an improved ability to ask the right questions and to know the wrong answers." What is more, he finds a comparable advantage in having instant access to the database to try out an idea he might have. In fact, he has a computer terminal at home and takes another with him on vacations.'

With these two models in mind, start by determining the management style of your CEO — is it more the Mintzberg model or the Heineman model? If it is the latter, probably no training program is necessary. But, I suspect that the Mintzberg model is more common. However, the style of your CEO could well be a combination of the two.

In addition, research indicates humans have different types of 'intelligences,' with different parts of the brain controlling different abilities. For example, we are so constituted that some of us learn better from pictures than from words.

Howard Gardner suggests there are six intelligences — linguistic, musical, logical-mathematical, spatial, bodily-kinesthetic and personal (Gardner 1983). Drawing on Gardner's work, Theodore Reid and Richard Dooley note that poets, writers and public speakers have exceptional linguistic skills; composers, conductors and musical performers have exceptional musical skills; engineers, mathematicians and computer programmers have exceptional logical-mathematical skills; artists, sculptors and architects have exceptional spatial skills; while athletes, mimes and dancers have exceptional bodily-kinesthetic skills. The sixth ability, personal intelligence, allows one to be in touch with one's own internal feelings as well as to notice and distinguish motivations and intentions in others. Those occupations where personal skills are important cover a wide gamut, but include diplomats, sales professionals, labour negotiators — and business executives (Reid and Dooley 1986).

Dr Reid correlates types of intelligence and effective computer-learning techniques. He claims that the logical-mathematical and the musical do best with programmed instruction; the linguistic with written documentation; the spatial where the overall picture is shared first and the various tasks overviewed; the bodily-kinesthetic with a hands-on, do-it-yourself, trial-and-error approach. Those with personal intelligence, most of the CEOs by the way, will learn more effectively with personal, individual, one-on-one instruction. While this is an oversimplification and it is apparent that most of us have more than one intelligence, the theory does seem to hold up in practice.

Though the business schools of our country may be turning out progressively more Ben Heinemans with enhanced logical-mathematical intelligence, my experience finds Mintzberg-model executives with strong personal skills to be the predominant model. Nonetheless, the first step is to establish the management style and intelligence characteristics of the CEO in question. It is useful to consider these differences in structuring learning techniques. In most cases, I predict the CEOs will be high in 'personal' skills, and a one-on-one, highly interactive mode of learning will be most effective.

2.4.2 Plan and conduct work sessions on the critical issues

Literacy is a value-charged, emotional term; it suggests its opposite — illiteracy — which is pejorative. However, as Ferdinand J. Setaro points out, everyone is illiterate when confronted with the technological blitz of the Information Era (Setaro 1986). He indicates that it may be more important to be aware of what you *do not* have to know — a kind of planned illiteracy. I share Mr Setaro's concern, because as an information systems professional who considers himself fairly well-informed, I sometimes feel I keep reading more and more and knowing less and less.

Nonetheless, the information systems 'content' described earlier is the starting point for attaining information literacy. The training should be accomplished in short spurts of an hour or two, built on a practical business related framework. What better way for the Information Systems Executive and the CEO to build a rapport than to share these periods, discussing critical areas of information system deployment within the company.

The most effective education may be when it's not called education. For example, on the topic of databases, the discussion might centre on why it is difficult to get key operating data to the senior staff in a timely manner. This would initiate a discussion of 'operational' databases, which are optimized to handle the thousands of transactions that take place each day. This is in distinct contrast to 'management' databases, which should be summarized data that is easy to retrieve. The importance for the CEOs to clearly define their information needs would also begin to surface.

In the area of telecommunications, the discussion might revolve around the benefits of an electronic mail system throughout the company. This would lead to a discussion of the trade-offs of different types of telecommunications facilities and the need to properly manage such facilities. These discussions should be given in six to eight modules over a period of two to three months. Selected short readings should be suggested as an adjunct.

The session logistics should be tailored to the CEO's schedule and mode of operation. Most CEOs have twelve-hour work days of 'wall-to-wall' meeting, with phone and individual enquiries punctuating the day. Somehow the information system executive must break into this agenda, to obtain an hour or two every week or so. The best approach is to schedule it as the first event of the day and away from the CEO's office, if at all possible. Also, there should be good use of visual aids, with the session objectives clearly stated. As has been mentioned, real-life situations with which the CEO is familiar should be used as illustrations. The more customary two- or three-day, one-shot seminar is less effective than the continued one- to two-hour modules which stress learning as a process, not an event.

2.4.3 Add computer literacy to information literacy

Information System tools are reducing the skills necessary to access and manipulate data. A provocative study by Benjamin M. Compaine projects a new literacy brought on by information technology. He states:

'The question behind the new literacy notion then is whether the use of compunications [computers and communication] will reduce the skills levels needed for certain types of problem solving and general information-seeking behaviour in society and at the same time make it necessary for this new level of skill to become an integral part of what it means to be "literate'" (Compaine 1984).

A key question for executives is at what juncture does it make sense to employ the tools directly rather than delegate their use? I have a professional working for me who is adept at using the graphic and symbol manipulation software of the Apple Macintosh to organize and develop consulting reports for clients. I am convinved that this ability enables him to create analyses, relationships among data, and unique meanings and presentation formats that materially improve the results.

The question I ask is: 'Since I have more consulting experience, can I use these tools myself to produce an even more insightful analysis for our clients?' But then, again, I wonder, 'Would I be doing something that rightfully should be delegated?'

Yet, I see my consultant improving both the 'medium *and* the message'. With tools getting progressively easier to use, is it time to take the plunge? If not the plunge, I feel it is at least time for executives to test the water. They should gain enough familiarity with personal computing to make their own decision on this issue − and it *is* a personal decision.

As with information literacy, to develop computer literacy the 'one-to-one' approach and the one- to two-hour slots should be employed. A simple word-processing program, spreadsheet or a database should serve the purpose. Selecting a reasonable learning tool is crucial, because CEOs will quickly lose interest if they have to grasp several dozen command or function codes. Again, the emphasis should be on the real world using actual company statistics or financial data. For example, data on product movement for the past two years can be accumulated by branch office, sales territory, key customer or product line. Then, with either a spreadsheet format or a fourth-generation language, data can be manipulated for reporting historical information or used to project future product or customer activity. This exposure is more meaningful after the relevant issues have been discussed, because the personal computer world is really a subset of the bigger corporate computer world; that is, you are dealing with data-bases, communications and end-user computing in both.

During these sessions, it will become clear whether the CEO will be a computer user personally or continue to delegate. Whichever the choice, however, the CEO is far better off with a new understanding and brief 'hands-on' exposure. If the CEO wants to go further, then an individual needs-assessment should be conducted and the necessary data compiled to provide the requisite management database. But it is crucial that the CEO decides personally whether the personal computer fits their management style; the decision comes by natural evolution, not by guilt or outside pressures.

2.5 CONCLUSION

Since its inception, Information Systems has borne the brunt of the problems caused by the proliferation of computer systems throughout the corporation. IS has been and will continue to be a 'problem' function. We are just beginning to understand that, in a complex environment, systems are indeed more than a combination of hardware, software and the people who implement them. End-users, including senior management and the CEO, are also vital parts of the system. They are part of the IS 'problem,' and are a key element in the 'solution'.

A first step is information literacy. The traditional approach has been to conduct a course on computer fundamentals and a 'hands-on' session on a personal computer. That is just not going to work. Typical CEOs are in their fifties, have reached their position without information literacy, and either think that it is too late to learn or that their involvement is irrelevant. By stressing *information* literacy, there is an opportunity to reach the CEO, approaching the task from a perspective that says 'you don't have to know how to repair a car to manage an automobile company, but you'd better realize the importance of quality, safety and economy in car production'. The analogy holds in Information Systems; knowing what computers can do and why they do it is mandatory; distinguishing a RAM from a ROM is optional.

REFERENCES

Compaine, B. M. (1984) *Information Technology and Cultural Change: Toward a New Literacy?* Cambridge, MA: Centre for Information Policy Research, Harvard University, Septembe.

Deardon, J. (1966) Myth of real-time management information, *Harvard Business Review*, May-June, pp. 123-128.

Deardon, J. (1972) MIS is a mirage, *Harvard Business Review*, January-February, pp. 90-99.

Deardon, J. (1983) Will the computer change the job of top management? *Sloan Management Review*, Fall, pp. 57-60.

Gardner, H. (1983) *Frames of Mind*, New York: Basic Books.

Honan, P. (1986) Captains of industry, *Personal Computing*, October, pp. 131-133.

Kepner-Tregoe, Inc. (1986) Top corporate execs think PCs are great — for everyone else, *Information Week*, May 19, p 61.

Mallach, E. G. (1986) The case against computer literacy, *Computerworld*, March 10, p 17.

Mintzberg, H. (1975) Folklore & fact, *Harvard Business Review,* July-August, pp. 43-49.

Reid, F. Theodore and Dooley, R. E. (1986) The challenge of multiple intelligences for the information executive, *Babson CIMS Working Paper Series*, December, pp. 9-12.

Rockart, J. F. (1982) The CEO goes on line, *Harvard Business Review,* January-February, pp. 82-88.

Setaro, F. J. (1986) The computer illiteracy measurement scale, *Babson CIMS Working Paper Series,* April, p 3.

Part Two

Executive Information Systems

3 Corporate policy and executive information

R. Matthews
Director of the Industrial Performance Unit
Director of EIS Consultants

3.1 INTRODUCTION

In the 1980s organizations experienced profound changes in their environments. Executives perceive that the pace of change is accelerating. The complexity of business has increased with the growth of the number of products and services produced in multiplying markets. Competition and pressures from financial markets have intensified. It is not surprising that these factors have brought changes in the information demands of organizations, one feature of which is the rapid growth of executive information systems (EIS). The 1990s will no doubt see more dramatic changes and place new requirements on information managers.

3.2 AIMS

The aims of this paper are to:

1. Describe a framework for understanding the role of information and executive information systems in organizations which has proved useful in research and consultancy.

2. Present new results of research into the use of EIS in leading companies in the UK.

3. Set out the implications of the framework and the research results for information executives in the 1990s.

The results described are based on research on executive information systems carried out by the Industrial Performance Unit at Kingston Business School from 1987 onwards.

3.3 FROM DATA TO INTELLIGENCE

Among the key findings of our research is the growing involvement of information managers in formulating corporate strategy. The technically oriented information executive is being replaced by one who is oriented towards management. Increasingly the information executive's role is to ensure that rapidly evolving technical opportunities are understood and acted upon. New opportunities bring about significant changes in organizations and an evolution in his or her job.

The information executive in large organizations no longer controls all computer-based activities. Frequently day-to-day line responsibility is devolved and the information executive takes on a staff role concerned with strategy, planning, monitoring performance, managing research into information systems and disseminating techniques and ideas rather than implementing them personally. The first 30 years of computer development can be termed the data processing era and the future will contain the information era (Rockart 1982; Earl 1989).

A number of factors are critical to understanding the problems of the relatively new role of information executives:

1. A gap exists between the skills and expertise of the traditional information executive and the information needs of the senior executives.

2. Essentially this gap is due more to misunderstandings of the needs of decision makers and the way in which management style causes variation in these needs than to corporate cultures which are resistant to new technology *per se.*

3. Generally information is not gathered which corresponds to the way in which organizations add value: it is driven by accounting requirements and delivered in a data processing mode. Decision makers require information linked to the value-creating activities of the organization.

4. Decision makers can have a profound capacity to ignore critical information. Clear indications were available to the retail sector in 1988-9 that inflationary pressures would force up interest rates, increasing the costs of debt and reducing consumer demand. This is but one example of many instances of corporate distress − in this case brought about through increased gearing and insufficient interest cover in the face of clear evidence of potential consequences before the event.

To understand these problems it is necessary to recognize that information is not cold and objective. It is useful to distinguish between data, information, perception and intelligence as set out in Figure 3.1.

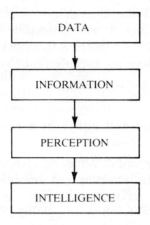

Fig. 3.1.

DATA. This is made up of all the available 'facts' about the organization and its environment.

INFORMATION. Data assembled in a systematic way becomes information which can be utilized by decision makers.

PERCEPTION. Information is processed by the perceptions of decision makers. Perceptions colour the nature of information received by decision makers in an organization.

INTELLIGENCE. Intelligence is the process through which the significance of information for achieving organizational goals in the future is recognized.

The transition of the information executive's role from the data processing era to the information era can be seen as an evolution in his or her concerns from data to intelligence. The role is not limited to assembling data in a systematic way. His or her concern now stretches to processing information in such a way that its significance can be understood. In turn this presupposes an understanding of management and leadership styles and the strategy of the organization.

3.4 THE MEANING OF ORGANIZATIONS

Why do organizations exist and how do they add value? The answer to the first question is that the existence of an organization can only be justified if it adds more value as an integral unit than it does as a set of independent parts. The answer to the second is that value is determined by the value of the projects which the organization undertakes.

A major concern of an organization is with providing information which is relevant to its goals and incentives to managers to act on the information. This view of an organization as an information system was expressed by Hayek (1930). Essentially the concern is to processing internal and external information so as to achieve the organizational goals of:

1. Achieving efficiency and/or profit.

2. Managing risks.

3. Learning to identify and adapt to a rapidly changing business environment.

These can be summarized as achieving competitive advantage which in the corporate sector means attaining and sustaining a rate of return above average for its industry or service group or risk class (Porter 1980 and 1982.)

Pressures of competition (often on a global scale) compel organizations in the corporate sector to achieve competitive advantage, but the process is a Schumpeterian one in which no organization can rest. Competitive advantage once achieved acts as a magnet attracting new competition. Competitive pressures are perceived by executives to be intense. (Schumpeter 1979). Similar pressures to those in the corporate sector are being placed on organizations which were traditionally non-profit-making, for example the NHS, Civil Service departments and local authorities.

Generally survival has come to depend on understanding exactly how value is generated, which projects contribute positively, which negatively and which are justified by the value that they add to other projects.

EIS fit into the latter category. Of themselves they are of little value; they generate value in so far as they provide critical information effectively in the sense that they add value to other activities. This is why it is so difficult to carry out investment appraisal of EIS in a conventional way. An important question surrounds what is meant by 'effectively' in this context.

3.5   EXECUTIVE INFORMATION SYSTEMS (EIS)

3.5.1   Understanding the present

Although this paper advocates change in the way we think about them, in many respects the business methodology of EIS is sounder than that underlying many planning models. Competitive advantage is not achieved by those companies which think of the future in terms of grand design but by those which are opportunistic. The future is not something to be minutely planned for, but it can be managed if executives have developed the right systems for understanding the present: that is, adequate systems for day-to-day control.

The future cannot be 'second guessed' as many economic and business planning models tend to assume, but it is possible to understand the present. This is the essential methodology behind EIS which is expressed through assigning control an equal partnership, with planning in the strategic planning process. EIS enable a feedback movement to be set up between planning and control through the 'moving present'. This is expressed in Figure 3.2.

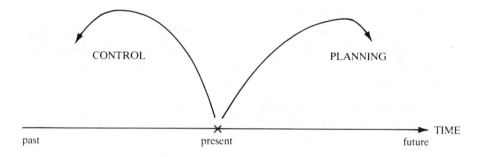

Fig. 3.2 The planning and control feedback.

3.5.2 EIS definition and aims

Rockart and Delong (1988) (preferring the term executive support system) define an executive information system as:

> 'the routine use of a computer-based system, most often through direct access to a terminal or personal computer, for any business function. The users are either the CEO or a member of the senior management team reporting directly to him or her. Executive support systems can be implemented at the corporate or divisional level.'

The use of EIS is evolving beyond board level. A much wider group of managers lower down in the hierarchy are becoming users and this represents a very considerable element of rapidly growing demand.

A distinction is frequently made in the literature between decision support systems and EIS. DSS offer standalone enquiry systems, analysis, modelling facilities for individual managers. Often designed and driven by themselves. Defined as soft technologies because the determinants of success or failure depend on non-technical factors such as problem orientation, evolutionary approach to systems design, and the systems analyst working as a process consultant rather than a provider of solutions.

EIS are more dependent on a range of technologies; computer terminals, on-line information services, database architectures. They provide internal information and a range of external information. EIS are defined in broad terms in this paper to include DSS applications.

According to Rockart and Delong, managerial applications of EIS can be viewed in two dimensions: function and purpose. The first dimension relates to the functions which managers perform and are made up of:

1. Communications-based applications including electronic mail and computer 'conferencing'.

2. Status access to a predetermined number of preformatted reports which are regularly updated. A hierarchy of menus allows movement from one report to another and enables the executive to monitor the performance of the organization regularly.

3. A capability to perform random and unstructured analysis of data or modelling can be created using fourth-generation tools or spreadsheet packages which may be linked to corporate databases.

The second dimension, the purpose for which systems are used, include:

1. Enhancing office efficiency through improved communications and access to information.

2. Improving the organization's planning and control systems through providing accurate and timely information which increases the efficiency of routine tasks. This in turn enables senior executives to focus on the ambiguous and often ill-defined problems for which they are responsible.

3.6   A STRATEGIC FRAMEWORK FOR EIS

Three forces must be reconciled by would-be providers of strategic information needs:

1. The opportunities and threats presented by the business environment. These are most frequently expressed through the actions of competitors.

2. The distinctive competencies of the organization which give it a comparative advantage. Competition will often require an organization to develop and adapt these competencies in a rapidly changing world.

3. The organization's management style and culture which frequently limits what it can achieve.

To achieve competitive advantage an organization needs to relate these three elements through its information system. In the 1980s a strategy was analysed in terms of either cost leadership or differentiation (responsiveness to customer needs often achieved through segmenting markets). Increasingly competitive pressures require that organizations achieve BOTH low cost and differentiation capabilities. Frequently culture and management style present the significant or even insuperable barrier to achieving these goals simultaneously.

To complicate their tasks further, in a rapidly changing business environment businesses are also required to become learning organizations capable of adapting to change and disseminating information effectively between members (Bartlett and Ghoshal 1989; Kanter 1989).

The diagram below (Figure 3.3) illustrates a framework for corporate strategy and successful EIS which has proved useful in numerous research and consultancy projects.

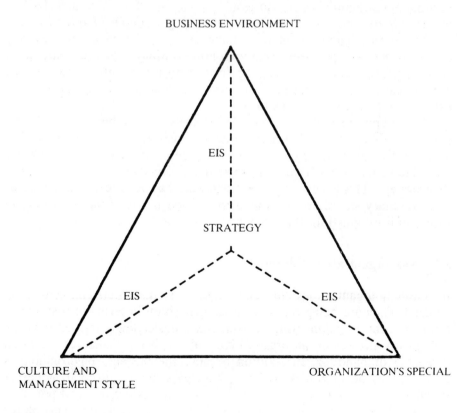

Fig. 3.3

3.7   RESEARCH FINDINGS ON EIS

3.7.1 Background

The framework provides a useful way of reporting some of the results of on going research and consultancy projects on executive information systems by the Industrial Performance Unit at Kingston Business School. The findings reported in this paper resulted from a number of projects on the relationship between EIS and corporate strategy carried out by the Unit between 1987 and 1990. These projects include:

- A survey based on the responses of 284 UK companies more than half of which had turnover exceeding 'drill-down' for detailed information in the company regardless of management style or of the way in which it characteristically added value.

Lack of awareness of the strategic competencies or the dependence of requirements on management style leaves an enormous gap in the information structure which can result in under-performance and the loss of markets to competitors. Philips is a striking example of this in recent months: senior management were unaware of performance because key competencies had not been clearly identified. Many examples exist in all sectors of the economy ranging from retail through to chemicals, automobiles and financial services and in companies purporting to have executive information systems in place.

This paper provides a triangular framework for building the most appropriate EIS which takes account of the organizational environment, its distinctive competencies and its management style. Traditionally information managers have concerned themselves with technology rather than strategy. This is changing. The framework has been tested in a number of consultancy situations and found to provide the information managers with useful insights into their new role.

3.7.2 New organizational demands

Increasingly organizations are being required to meet new and conflicting demand. They are being required to compete both in terms of cost and in terms of differentiation (which is sometimes misleadingly termed quality). This places stresses on an organization which existing structures are often incapable of handling. In addition because the business environment is perceived to be extremely volatile, managers are required to generate learning organizations in which information flows effectively and potential synergies between business units or projects can be exploited. This places new requirements on EIS. The spread of EIS to lower levels in the hierarchy is an early stage in the process of creating intelligent organizations capable of learning.

3.7.3 The EIS product cycle

The market for EIS is rapidly growing. Some estimates put the growth of expenditures at around 35% in 1991: our estimates are nearer 20% growth: the difference perhaps results from the relatively high level of 'in-house' investments.

Development in many companies tends to be *ad hoc*. Investment appraisal is largely carried out on a subjective basis. Post-audit of investments is relatively rare except among companies with above-average experience with IT investments in general and EIS in particular, e.g. the oil majors.

If EIS investments follow the trend of other IT expenditures then in the next phase of expansion companies will begin to place more emphasis on the control and evaluation of expenditures than they are currently doing. Hard savings will be sought. Both financial and quality controls will be enforced (Earl 1989).

3.7.4 Competitive pressures and EIS

The main role of EIS is to deliver information which is relevant to the way in which the organization adds value. This entails breaking an organization into a set of projects (which may be interdependent) and generating information which enables projects to be monitored. Indications are that (in an increasingly competitive environment) unless the organization itself is capable of achieving this then either its competitive advantage will be eroded by rivals in the marketplace, or successful predators will arise in the form of rival management teams acting through the stock market.

Hence the question to ask in designing an EIS is: What information would potential predators most like to have about your organization?

REFERENCES

Bartlett, C. A. and Ghoshal, S. (1989) *Managing Across Borders*. Hutchinson, London.

Earl, M. J. (1989) *Management Strategy for Information Technology*. Prentice-Hall, UK.

Fatmi, H. A. (1971) An approach towards understanding the psycho-physiological mechanism of perception and awareness, in *Biokybernetik*. Veb Gustav Fischer Verlag, Jena.

Goold, M. and Campbell, A. (1987) *Strategies and Styles*. Basil Blackwell, Oxford.

Hayek, F.A. Von (1949) The use of knowledge in society, in *Individualism and the Economic Order*. Routledge & Kegan Paul, London.

Kanter, R. M. (1989) *When Giants Learn to Dance*. Simon & Schuster, New York.

Lowles, T. L. and Matthews, R. (1990) *Executive Information Systems*. Kingston Business School.

Matthews, R. (1987) *Directors' Information Systems*. Metapraxis, Kingston upon Thames.

Porter, M. E. (1980) *Competitive Strategy*. Free Press, New York.

Rockart, J. F. (1982) The changing role of the information executive. *Sloan Management Review*.

Rockart, J. F. (1988) *Executive Support Systems*. Dow Jones-Irwin, Illinois.

Round, A. R. and Sheppard, J. (1990) *Executive Information Systems: An examination of their strategic value*. Kingston Business School.

Schumpeter, J. A. (1979) *Capitalism, Socialism and Democracy*. Allen & Unwin, London.

4 What top managers want from EIS in the 1990s

C. Holtham
City University Business School

SYNOPSIS

This paper covers two inter-related areas. It firstly outlines a research programme led by the author into the direct use of IT by company directors. The paper then examines the specific topic of Executive Information Systems. It concludes by identifying three areas where executive information systems need to be augmented if they are to be more effective in meeting directors' needs in the 1990s.

4.1 THE DIRECT USE OF I.T. BY COMPANY DIRECTORS

4.1.1 The problem

Many organizations are failing to make the link between information technology and business strategy. Many of the present generation of top managers and company directors have developed their knowledge and understanding of IT in an *ad hoc* fashion. Previous research at City University Business School suggested that the intuitive feel needed to capitalize on modern information technology is often lacking (Holtham 1989). It is essential that top managers cannot only react to IT initiatives from middle managers, but are themselves confident both in the basics of IT, and in the opportunities provided by leading-edge applications of IT in business. We believe there is a greater leadership role possible by top managers relating to the effective use of IT. It is also necessary to open up to top managers the opportunities afforded by the application of technology to learning in a practical business context. In certain areas of business the effective application of learning technology is becoming a strategic issue, and that there is an urgent need to enable top managers to be aware of the opportunities available in this specific area.

There also needs to be a recognition of the importance of 'Information Management', which can be defined as follows: '... companies will seek to use their information systems to help them react more quickly, to get them closer to their customers, to their suppliers, to their distributors and to their contractors. In other words, organizations will use information strategically.'

This needs to be sharply contrasted with the information technology — hardware and software — which is used to deliver these aims. There is too great a concentration on IT, and insufficient emphasis on information management.

In order to address these problems, the Institute of Directors and the Business School obtained funding from the Training Agency for a project on 'Director and senior management awareness of IT for business success'. This involves both research and the development of solutions to deal with this type of problem. It began in late 1989 and was scheduled to be concluded by the autumn of 1991.

4.1.2 The project

The central core of the project is the design and production of PC-based courseware which is explicitly oriented to the needs of top managers and to the effective use of IT in business. Such courseware will be particularly attractive if available on an easily portable laptop PC which the top manager can, in particular, use at home or during the course of their travels.

Research into the nature of top managerial work has shown that the top manager is often addressing many issues simultaneously, is often highly mobile geographically and has relatively short periods of time available for focusing on specific issues. There is also evidence of some resistance to the idea of 'training' for top managers, particularly in the area of IT. The nature of top management work is also very diverse between different organizations depending on ownership, size, structure and style. It has therefore been essential to devise an approach to learning which:

1. Is sufficiently attractive to attract and sustain the interest of the top manager
2. Is sufficiently flexible to be relevant to a reasonable range of managerial situations.

4.1.3 Project aims

There are three interrelated objectives:

1. To inform, stimulate and even excite senior managers and company directors about the possibilities and potential of IT for their businesses.

2. To promote with this key group of decision makers the whole concept of computerized training and information, through their own hands-on use of IT.

3. To evaluate alternative methods of delivery to the senior manager.

It is well established that this group has in general problems with or aversions to use of conventional PCs. Some of the barriers identified are:

- Fear of personal innovation
- Slowness of learning curve
- Inadequacy of human computer interface
- Lack of portability of output
- Structured nature of data
- Beliefs about the top management role
- Lack of input by top managers to systems design
- Perceived cost

4.1.4 Evaluation of potentially relevant technology

It is often argued that the keyboard is a barrier to executive use. Part of the project has evaluated some new and innovative technologies, particularly in the input/output area, both for their relevance in course delivery to this group and to their acceptability to participants for use in an office environment.

These have included:

1. Portable computers

2. Pocket computers

3. Telephone dial systems

4. Compact-disk ROM (portable)

5. Still and moving video on PCs

6. Touch screens

7. 'Soft', reconfigurable keyboards

8. Voice input and output

9. The PC pedal

From our initial evaluation the three most promising technologies to improve or enhance executive use of IT are:

- the pocket computer
- TV and video on the PC
- voice input

CD-ROM offers great potential for courseware delivery, especially for image and video work, and now simply awaits the benefits of mass marketing pricing to take off.

4.1.5 Research into top management awareness

This research has been carried out by:

1. Identifying the key barriers to top management awareness of IT.
2. Investigating particular features of top management training and learning.
3. Interviewing top managers who have become successfully aware of IT, and who either use it or promote its use .
4. Interviewing top managers who are currently unaware of IT.

This research feeds directly into the structure and design of the courseware, as well as leading to a project report.

4.1.6 Contents of final report and dissemination arrangements

There will be several outputs from the project:

1. Courseware
   - Learning Guide
   - Computer Delivered Activities
2. Director's Advisor
   - Computer-based checklist/expert system
3. Research into IT awareness and needs of top managers/directors
   - Research Report
4. Overall Project Report
   - Summarizing the separate outputs
   - Extent of achievement of objectives
   - Indications of promising areas for future development.

The courseware and Directors' Guide will be marketed and published by the Institute of Directors.

4.1.7 Emerging points

Some of our preliminary conclusions are:

1. There is much more interest in the personal use of IT by company directors than we had suspected from previous surveys into their usage levels.

2. There are a number of very clear barriers to their personal use:
   - Lack of suitable training
   - Poor support and documentation

   but above all:

   - Lack of relevant systems

3. Directors' requirements vary considerably, not only between but also within organizations.

4. There is a very significant difference between usage and interest levels in smaller as opposed to larger organizations.

5. We believe there is some linkage between directors' personal use of IT and the strategic impact of IT in the organization.

The one type of software that has been explicitly designed for top managers and directors is executive information systems software, and the following section evaluates the extent to which the current generation of EIS are likely to make a fundamental impact on directors' information needs.

4.2 INFORMATION FOR MANAGERS AND EIS

The City University Business School has taken a close interest in EIS over the last two years and in that time has carried out eight studies of EIS application, virtually all on a contract basis for individual clients, ranging from developing a prototype EIS for banks to a review of the external information sources for a public utility.

The school has also developed an innovative MBA course in 'Improving Managerial Productivity', which has been extremely well supported by practitioners from EIS vendors, consultants and users. This section draws on this broad range of work.

4.2.1 Information managers say what they want

When surveyed, a common response to the question of what information they use is as shown in the following table:

Type of information used by senior managers	% using
Sales	85
Budgets/Forecasts	83
Market Trends	37
External Information	35
Economic Data	35
Competitor Activity	30
Other	30
	(Romtec, 1988)

There tends to be an equation of information needs with formal and even quantitative type information. Yet studies such as Mintzberg's into the actual behaviour of top managers has suggested many intuitive roles as well as those requiring formal quantitative information.

Interpersonal Roles
Figurehead
Leader
Liaison

Informational Roles
Monitor
Disseminator
Spokesman

Decisional roles
Entrepreneur
Disturbance Handler
Resource Allocator

4.2.2 Negotiator managerial roles (Mintzberg 1973)

The current generation of EIS make relatively little impact on these twelve roles, although for those that it does serve it is an improvement over what has often preceded it.

There is one line of argument that could be developed to challenge EIS based on formal data, for example that set out by Peters (1989) in a more general context:

'Our fixation with financial measures leads us to downplay or ignore less tangible non-financial measures, such as product quality, customer satisfaction, factory flexibility, the time it takes to launch a new product, and the accumulation of skills by labour over time. Yet these are increasingly the real drivers of corporate success over the middle to long term.'

In fact some of Peters' critical success factors are quantifiable, even if not financially based, but in general appear in only a minority of EIS implementations to date, at least in the UK (Holohan 1990).

If features of a successful EIS are accepted as summarized in Rockart and DeLong (1988), namely that it:

- changes and enhances the way the manager thinks about the business;
- improves the manager's mental model of the firm;
- provides the manager with better planning and control capabilities;
- makes better use of the manager's time;
- educates the manager about the use and potential of information technologies;

then it would appear the present financial and hard data orientation of most UK EIS's fit them well for the 'planning and control' role, but less well for some of the other features, particularly the second one. This is best facilitated by approaches that do not simply allow drilling down (and up) a formal pyramid of data, but which also take inputs from outside and the future on a much greater scale than is currently done.

There is considerable scope to draw on operational research and statistical thinking and methods to a much greater extent than before, and also to take on board emerging thinking from the knowledge-based systems world, as well as that of both cybernetics and soft systems methodologies.

It appears that the present type of EIS is rooted in:

1. Summarized management accounting systems.

2. The application of attractive but limited graphics and user interface on the top manager's desk.

3. Text, numbers.

It is really often a conventional MIS or MAS re-packaged, and this in part explains some of the implementation problems, especially where it has been oversold internally and externally.

There will be a 'next-generation' of EIS. It should be noted that the phrases 'second-generation EIS' and even 'third-generation EIS' have already been hypothecated by the marketing departments of some EIS vendors. The next-generation will not just re-structure existing hard data and attractively re-present it. It will also attack:

1. The whole issue of soft data and multiple media including image, video, voice etc.

2. The changing nature of critical success factors, especially in fast-moving images.

3. The failure of EIS formally to address the collective decision-making process.

4. The need to embed information in a philosophy of use of information and an organizational context for its use.

So to summarize, the next-generation EIS will tend to reflect:

- A move beyond 'data processing' into a multi-media framework.
- A greater emphasis on the conceptual model of the enterprise used.
- A greater capability for using and applying operational research and statistical approaches.

4.3 CONCLUSION

Rockart and Delong (1988) reached a number of conclusions from their research into EIS that have largely been borne out from our own work:

1. ESS is just emerging from the pioneering stage and must be treated in this context.

2. It is just one tool in the armament of senior managers. Much of the work done by senior managers will receive at best marginal support from ESS.

3. ESS are not for everyone in the next few years.

4. Office support, especially electronic mail and planning and control systems, will continue to be the prime uses of ESS, since communications and control are managerial 'musts'.

5. The ultimate payoff (and the real benefit for planning and control) is the enhanced understanding of the business environment these systems can provide for top managers.

6. Widespread use of ESS will not happen overnight. But it is inevitable.

We are probably less optimistic in relation to conclusion 6, at least in the UK. We are also not optimistic in the medium term about the direct managerial use of office support systems.

REFERENCES

Business Intelligence (1989) The EIS report, second edition, Business Intelligence, London.

Dockery, E. (1990a) The use of information systems in managerial work: perspectives on directors, chief executives, and senior management use of computers, City University Business School Working Paper.

Dockery, E. (1990b) The strategic use of information systems technology in banking firms and building society organizations, City University Business School Working Paper.

EOSYS (1986) Top executives and information technology — disappointed expectations, EOSYS, Slough.

Holohan, J. (1990) EIS: Identifying key performance indicators, EIS Forum Report, Business Intelligence, London.

Holtham, C. (1989) IT systems for top management, *Information Management Yearbook*, pp. 148-151, IDPM, London.

Martin, C. (1988) Computers and senior managers, National Computing Centre, Manchester.

Matthews, R. (1988) The boardroom revolution, Metapraxis Ltd, Kingston upon Thames.

Mintzberg, H. (1973) *The Nature of Managerial Work*, Harper & Row, New York.

Peters, T. (1989) Thriving on chaos.

Rajan, A. (1988) Information technology and managers: some good practices, Institute of Manpower Studies Report No. 146, Brighton.

Rockart, J. F. and Delong, D. W. (1988) *Executive Support Systems,* Dow Jones-Irwin, Homewood, Illinois.

Romtec (1988) An assessment of the use and awareness of executive information systems, Romtec, Maidenhead, for Comshare.

Part Three

Group Decision Support Systems

5 Strategy development and implementation

The Role of a Group Decision Support System and 'EIS'

C. Eden and F. Ackermann
Strathclyde Business School, University of Strathclyde

'I believe ... that in deciding where you would like to be, as opposed to where you are probably going to end up, you need a great deal of discussion and a great deal of development of new thinking and new processes. The idea of doing this through the planning department, or through a paper on strategy presented to the board, seems to me to be quite inadequate. This process involves large amounts of time and constant discussion with those involved lower down the line who will actually execute the strategies on which the whole picture relies. This sort of circular debate, frequently widening out to involve others within and without the company, goes on until all are satisfied that the result is as good as they are going to get.' John Harvey-Jones (1988).

This paper is about the role of computers and special-purpose computer software in facilitating the type of discussion Harvey-Jones talks about. The role of the computer is twofold − to help groups in the organization with the discussion of strategy through the provision of a group decision support system (GDSS), and to provide members of the executive team with a sort of executive information system which can help with the implementation of strategy.

One of the greatest difficulties facing the Chief Executive involved in creating a sound strategy for their organization is not the development of the strategy but rather making the strategy have any real impact throughout the organization. The resolution of the difficulty rarely lies in making the strategy more correct from the point of view of its content, but one of gaining commitment, ownership and appropriate strategic control. The key lies in being able fundamentally to change strategic thinking in the organization. 'Decision conferencing' (Phillips 1990) and other group

This paper is a modified and extended version of a former paper to be published in R. Bostrom and S. Kinney (eds) (1992) New Directions in Group Decision Support, Von Nostrand Reinhold, New York.

decision support systems, such as that reported in this paper, are making progress through locking together the processes of strategy development and implementation. That is, computer- and facilitator-aided group processes are allowing more data to be carefully managed within the context of the sort of group activities that promote higher levels of ownership. The strategy is more robust because it has absorbed more of the experience, wisdom and judgements of a wider cross-section of the organization (up to 200 managers). Yet their participation in an overtly analytical process for dealing with their wisdom and the consequent belief that they have had an opportunity to influence the strategy generates high levels of ownership. Importantly, by bringing to the surface the realities as seen by those further down the organization, it not only provides ownership but counters the risks of locked-in perspectives that derive from the 'mind of the organization' at the top.

'One reason why you should try to develop the direction in which you think the company should go from both ends of the company at once is that in the process you gain the commitment of those who will have to follow the direction — and "make it happen" — and in a free society you are unlikely to get this commitment without a high degree of involvement and understanding of both where the ultimate goal is, and the process by which the decisions regarding that goal have been reached.' John Harvey-Jones (1988).

Returning to the introductory quote, this paper will now consider some of the characteristics of strategy development. In the light of these characteristics it will consider the role of computer assistance (group decision support) — specifically the role of a method known as Strategic Options Development and Analysis (SODA) (Ackermann 1990) and special purpose software (COPE) (Cropper, Eden and Ackermann 1990) which allows a group to 'play with' their ideas about strategy through the real-time interaction with graphical computer representations and analyses of their data. In addition the paper discusses how the computer model constructed to support groups becomes an executive support system to the process of strategic control.

The paper will also discuss some of the prerequisites for the successful use of group decision support systems and executive information systems in organizations.

5.1 THE NATURE OF STRATEGY DEVELOPMENT

Strategy development usually involves some or all of the following group activities:

- articulating strategic vision

- identifying major strategic issues facing the organization
- option generation and scenario building
- identification of stakeholders and their possible response in relation to their own goals.

These activities represent the groundwork of strategy building, followed by:

- developing an appropriate goal system for the organization
- setting strategies within the context of the goal system
- establishing a series of strategic programmes related to the strategies and representing an action package
- the creation of a mission statement in relation to the above
- developing a strategic control system involving a review of strategic performance and the performance of strategy.

If attention is paid to the major problems of implementing strategy — making it work for the organization — then these processes often involve large numbers of staff within the organization. Indeed it is typical for our own work with organizations, in both the private and public sectors, to use a cascading series of strategy workshops that might involve upwards of 200 staff. At several stages the senior executive team will come together to evaluate and analyse the content generated by these workshops. Sometimes the executive team may work with the output of 10-20 workshops, on other occasions it may involve working only with the content generated by the executive team themselves.

This continuing process of strategy development and review is depicted by Figures 5.1 and 5.2. Figure 5.1 shows the conceptual relationship between the different parts of strategy; the mission statement at the centre of a hierarchy of supporting strategies, each of which contains a system of strategic objectives or goals, which are in turn supported by a system of strategic programmes which locate portfolios of actions. The strategy is thus a hierarchical system of interacting and interrelating 'means' and 'ends', where each 'means' may impact on multiple 'ends'. Some 'ends' can be conceptualized as a strategy (key goal) — 'take risks with people earlier', a strategic objective (goal) — 'ensure acquisitions match staff expectations', or a strategic programme — 'reduce risks of jeopardizing careers'.

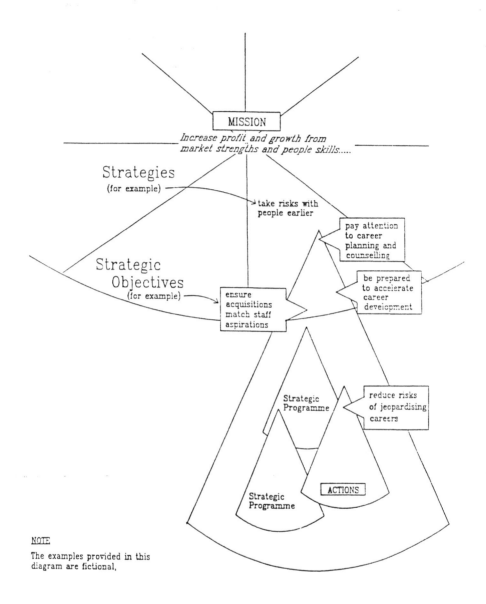

MISSION

Increase profit and growth from market strengths and people skills.....

Strategies
(for example)

take risks with people earlier

pay attention to career planning and counselling

Strategic Objectives
(for example)

ensure acquisitions match staff aspirations

be prepared to accelerate career development

Strategic Programme

reduce risks of jeopardising careers

ACTIONS

Strategic Programme

NOTE

The examples provided in this diagram are fictional.

Fig. 5.1 Schematic diagram representing the relationship between mission, strategies, strategic objectives and strategic programmes.

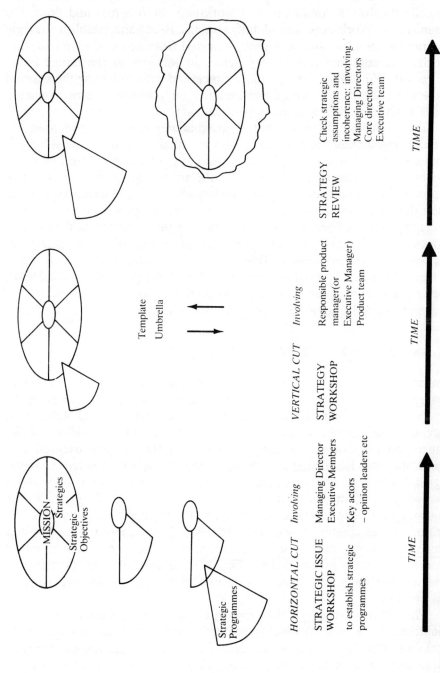

Fig. 5.2 The continuing process of strategic management.

Figure 5.2 shows how the process of strategy development and review typically involves a combination of workshops both across and down the organization. Workshops that identify strategic issues and establish strategic programmes tend to involve a group selected from across the organization (horizontal cut) and involve key actors in relation to the issues to be addressed. Workshops that are more concerned with collecting the wisdom and experience of staff lower down the line tend to involve a team associated with particular products or tasks (vertical cut).

The executive team is central to whatever processes are used for strategy development and it is they who are likely to gain the most benefit from computer-aided Group Decision Support. This paper describes some aspects of the use of SODA and COPE to provide such support. The approach has been used in a wide variety of different formats depending upon the nature of the organization – culture, personal style of the Chief Executive, level of sophistication in strategic management, and time and money available. The support system has been used within organizations such as Reed International (Eden, Ackermann and Timm 1990), Shell (Eden 1990a), BT, Prison Service (Eden, Cropper and Train 1990), Government departments, NHS (Telford, Ackermann and Cropper 1990), and multi-organizational settings (Pizey and Huxham 1989).

5.2   SODA AND COPE AS A GDSS AND 'EIS'

The conceptual framework described above is founded upon the notion that strategy development is about discovering how to manage and control the future. It is concerned with capturing the experience and wisdom of organizational members about how they believe an attractive vision of the future can be attained. Strategic thinking is thus action-oriented and concerned with identifying how to intervene in the incrementalism of the organization itself and its relationship with the environment. It is about discovering the 'means' that can create desired 'ends'. The data is the outcome of managers thinking about the future, and thinking about the future involves creating new theories (Spender 1989) about the relationship between the organization and its environment. These theories are based on experience and wisdom rather than precise forecasts or quantitative analyses. Judgements are made about how the market and the organization will be working.

The data of strategic thinking will, therefore, be dominated by a qualitative belief system which represents 'theories' about why the world works and thus how it can be changed. The need to recognize the complex interaction between the multiple beliefs of organizational members reflects the reality of every goal being qualified by others and every strategy being constrained and enhanced by a network of other strategies.

5.2.1 SODA and the discovery of a strategic belief system

As indicated above, the process of collecting experience and wisdom is through a series of workshops. Usually each involves between 6 and 24 people who will be invited to influence the strategy of the organization through the identification of strategic issues and emerging goals.

The Group Decision Support System is generally a combination of 'nominal group techniques' (Delbecq, Van de Ven and Gustafson 1975), the use of 'dominos/sno-cards' (Eden et al. 1983; Backoff and Nutt 1988), and the use of the COPE software for recording, analysis and display purposes. Participants work in groups of 6-10 people and are encouraged to use 'dominos' (20x10cm cards shaped as ellipses) to record and display their own views of the strategic issues facing the organization within the context of the views of other members of the group.

As participants display their ellipses on the wall in front of them they are continuously organized by the facilitator, with help from participants, into clusters of related statements. They are also implicitly arranged by the facilitator into an hierarchically arranged means/ends structure so that the most superordinate end is at the top and the most detailed means or option at the bottom of the cluster. Each cluster of statements represents an emerging 'strategic issue' identified by the group. The group members are encouraged to elaborate and contradict the emerging view of issues that are being created on the wall. Figure 5.3 shows an example of a developing cluster.

The clusters, their content, the interrelationship between content within clusters, and between clusters is recorded using the computer software. This is simply a record of a means/ends hierarchy — assertions about the future and their consequences. In practice the recorder will modify what is written on the ellipses in order that the assertion indicates an intervention to change the world — that it suggests a 'call to action'. The software records each statement as a numbered concept and records the linkage between concepts in the form of a directed graph (concepts as nodes linked together by arrows). Figure 5.4 shows a cluster being recorded and represented on the computer screen. The record of material generated during this early stage of issue identification is not classified into goals, strategies, actions etc., but rather remains as raw data (the computer record is in the default typeface and colour — yellow).

Fig. 5.3 An example of a 'domino' cluster.

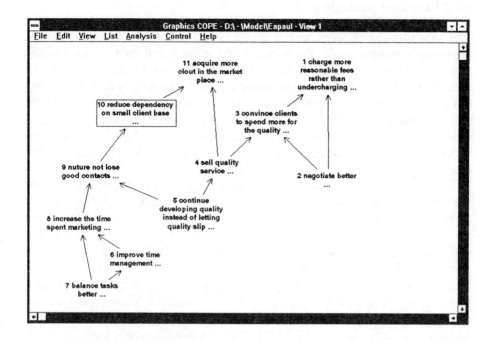

Fig. 5.4 A cluster recorded by COPE.

The request to focus on issues is designed to grab the attention of participants by allowing them to express 'firefighting' concerns (Eden 1990b) they each have about the future. This may promote a temptation to continually refer to the present (and thus past) nature of the world as it is expressed by the 'corporate rain-dance' of the annual planning process, rather than make explicit theories that are genuinely prospective. However, the use of dominos to record discussion is aimed at encouraging individuality whilst developing creativity and synergy alongside synthesis and reducing the probability of 'group-think'.

Focusing on strategic issues rather than the development of idealized scenarios or preferred goals is deliberately designed to ensure that strategy becomes something more than 'motherhood and apple pie'. The clusters are specific theories that apply to the world of the participants' specific organization rather than to any organization. It also reduces the possibility of participants discussing 'espoused theories' derived from attendance of management courses, rather than the 'theories of action' that will drive future decision making (Argyris 1983; Bartunek and Moch 1987).

5.2.2 Emerging strategic goals

The second stage of work with a group is focused on the identification of emerging strategic goals. Participants are encouraged to take an holistic view of each cluster and consider the goals that are implicit through the identification of a cluster as a strategic issue. When members of the group have emotionally and psychologically envisioned issues that must be resolved, then they will be implicitly or subconsciously presuming a desired direction for the organization. This stage of the workshop is designed to make explicit these assumptions about direction — hence they are the emerging strategic goals of the organization.

These goals are usually written onto 'post-its' (to differentiate them from the issue content) and are organized hierarchically in relation to each cluster in turn. It is at this stage that the clusters become explicitly related to one another, for each goal informs others, some of which are superordinate, thus relating to several clusters. The software is used to record these goals (which are coded differently within COPE — usually coloured white, made bold and given a larger typeface compared with issue statements). Through the large amount of material generated and the cross-linkages being collated into a single model, the group will now become increasingly dependent upon COPE and the computer display to manage the complexity of their strategy development. Thus the display can be used to focus upon any part of the model and show its linkage upwards to superordinate 'ends' and downwards to subordinate 'means'. Attention of the group gradually shifts from material on the wall to the aggregated model on the computer display. Thus the group absorbs the use of computer-aided group support in a 'natural' rather than directed manner. The use of the computer appears obvious and transparent.

5.2.3 Completing the groundwork of strategy development in groups

The stages listed at the beginning of the paper continue, but with greater emphasis on direct record of discussion into the computer software. Thus the group is encouraged to consider those statements that are most subordinate, within the strategic issues, as possible strategic options. The software is used to help locate potential options that might be particularly significant. For example, not all of the most subordinate concepts need be considered in the first instance, those that have a single chain of ramifications are likely to be less important than those with many ramifications. The software finds those potential options that are either 'potent' or 'key' (potent options are those that have ramifications for a large number of goals, key options are options that are most subordinate within the model having more than one consequence). As the group addresses these possible options they are encouraged to develop 'actionable' means to resolving the strategic issue being considered and so add new concepts to the model. As possible strategic options are identified they are given a typeface/colour that will clearly indicate them on the computer display, on a printout and as an analysable set within the model.

Similarly the possible reaction of stakeholders to 'key options' are noted within the model, both as responses that could damage or support the strategy and as stakeholder goals that might encourage them to respond in the manner predicted.

5.2.4 Refining strategy

The stages described above may be undertaken many times with a variety of groups within the organization. When working with any specific group a choice will be made about whether they are to build their own model of issues, goals, options and stakeholder responses or whether it is appropriate to aggregate their views with those recorded from previous groups. The choice is mostly resolved by considering the time available to work with the increased complexity of an aggregated model set against the potential for increased ownership of a broad organizational perspective on strategic issues.

Although it is possible for the executive team to consider the model after the backroom work of aggregating the material has been carried out, it is not possible for the groups generating the material to work with it all unless the software can be used in 'real-time'. This is especially true if a series of groups are working on the material as they will not only want to be able to review what previous groups have contributed but add their own comments and insights directly to it. Thus using 'real-time' software will enable them to grasp hold of the direction of other groups whilst adding their own. This facility also enables the executive team to work on the material interactively if they should so choose.

Whichever route has been chosen, the executive team will come together to consider a large amount of qualitative data — typically 1000-1500 concepts, made up of 40-50 issues, 80-90 potential goals and 200-300 potential strategic options. Their task, with the help of two facilitators and the computer support, is to refine the goal system, agree appropriate strategies to meet these goals, evaluate options and create a programme of action to support the strategies, and so write a mission statement that will act as an inspiration to members of the organization.

Two facilitators are used so that one facilitator can act mostly as a 'process-manager' in front of the group and the second facilitator act predominantly as a 'content-manager' in front of two computer screens (one screen working as a preview for the main screen refresh or for exploratory analysis). The large screen used by the group is either the display from a three-colour projector, or a large 37" colour EGA monitor. With one facilitator paying attention to process and the other to content it becomes possible to allow the analysis of content to be contingent upon the social processes of the group and the social processes of the group to be contingent upon the analysis of content (Eden 1990c). The facilitators are able to act in concert, and the social needs of the group and content of the issue are also able to be in concert with one another so that effective negotiation occurs (Eden 1989a).

The Group Decision Support task in relation to the executive team is to provide help in the management of complexity. COPE is designed to provide this help in a number of ways:

- each of the different categories of data, or all of the data, can be identified and displayed separately
- clusters can be formed where concepts are grouped so that there is a minimum number of bridging links to other clusters, thus identifying manageable parts of the model and suggesting emerging features of the strategy
- clusters can be formed based upon an hierarchical analysis of the model, thus sets can be formed which relate to particular parts of the goal system, allowing the exploration of possible strategic programmes
- particular parts of the model can be chosen to depict an overview by 'collapsing' the overall model down to, for example, the relationship between key options and certain goals
- 'central' concepts can be isolated through a sequence of analyses which identify those concepts with a dense domain of other concepts, or alternatively highly elaborated support (subordinate chains of 'means' to a selected 'end').

These analyses allow the structure of the strategy model to be explored so that the emerging characteristics of the data can be identified. It is through the 'playful' use of the model in this way that the executive team is able to get a feel for the model as a whole. Subsequently the team is able to focus on the task of reducing the goal system down to a manageable size — about 10-12 core strategic goals (strategies) supported by 15-20 other goals (strategic objectives). The process is a combination of analysing goal centrality with merging of goal statements to capture the essential features, of maybe four adjacent goal statements, into one goal (this merging process is easily managed with the help of the software, so that all interrelationships are maintained). Figures 5.5 and 5.6 show a typical merging of three goals. The process is cyclical, involving various analyses to provide an agenda of displays. These displays are focusing on 'central' concepts and subsequent rewording, merging and 'deleting' (concepts are never deleted in practice but rather reduced in typeface size and coloured deep blue so they become insignificant; this is because they sometimes resurface as significant as the cycle proceeds).

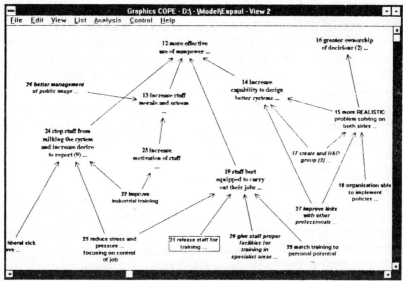

Fig. 5.5 A part of a goal map prior to merging.

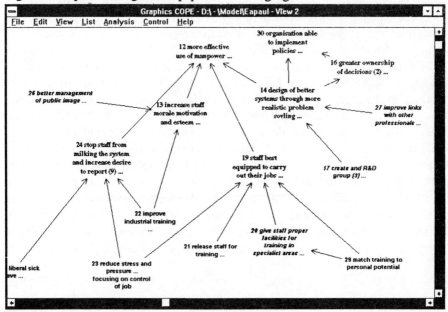

Fig. 5.6 A part of a goal map after merging.

An executive team seems able to make use of the support system with remarkable ease. They quickly become accustomed to the power of the software so that facilitation shifts from highly directed conceptual and technical guidance to collaborative support. The use of the computer mouse within a 'Windows' environment allows members of an executive team to grab control of the software so that the GDSS is transparent rather than technical 'magic'. Figure 5.7 shows an executive team at work.

Gradually the model is refined so that its form follows the conceptual categories shown by Figure 5.1, and the model typically is reduced to 150-200 concepts. The model contains the strategy of the organization which may be presented as 10-12 interlocked strategies. It is not unusual for the presentation of the strategy to all participating managers to be made using COPE projected onto a large screen, although it is usually helpful for a printed version of the core elements to be issued as an overview.

5.2.5 COPE as an 'EIS'

The strategy model developed by multiple groups and refined by the executive team is the agenda for strategic action. For it to be successfully implemented an effective strategic control system is absolutely essential (Goold and Quinn 1990). While a significant element of strategic control is the process of strategy review on a regular six-month and twelve-month basis (Eden, Ackermann and Timm 1990) a fundamental element is the problem-solving support the strategy framework is expected to provide executives on a day-to-day basis. In this respect the model is used in a variety of forms as a type of EIS.

Firstly the model resides on the personal computer of senior staff as the basis for 'problem framing', resource acquisition, acquisition and new product evaluation, and as the basis for 'vertical cut' in relation to task groups (Figure 5.2). Strategic control is established through the requirement that all requests for major decisions must be made by direct reference to the strategy model; by so doing decisions are more likely to be coherent in relation to the detail of strategy and in relation to one another. This corresponds with Turban's (1988) characteristics that 'EIS's principle use is in tracking and control'. A strategy that cannot be referred to in its full complexity allows decisions to be justified against strategy statements that are so superordinate, and therefore 'motherhood', they are open to multiple interpretations to suit the needs of the manager requesting resources.

Fig. 5.7 An executive team working with COPE.

Secondly the model becomes the basis for the review of all subordinate staff. Agreed strategic actions are recorded in the model with respect to the manager responsible for delivery and the date of delivery thus meeting another EIS requirement that the 'current state of performance in each area should be continually measured' (Rockart 1979). All managers are able to use COPE to search for all actions designated to a particular individual or team and not only check on progress but much more importantly check that progress is being designed to achieve the ends that the strategy originally determined. It is common for individual managers to claim successful implementation of a particular strategic action without undertaking the task in such a manner that the strategic aims of the action are achieved. COPE forces such considerations simply because all displays of actions show the supporting actions and expected consequences (Figure 5.8) — the manager is expected to demonstrate the attainment of the consequential arrows as well as the action itself. The review process is not restricted to the use of the model to check implementation of detailed actions but also as a part of the annual performance review of senior staff. Here the model becomes a structured prompt for asking staff to explain their performance and the performance of their staff in building the strategic future of the organization thus supporting Burkan's view, 'it is precisely in this regard [the review] that EISs can be such an invaluable aid' (1988).

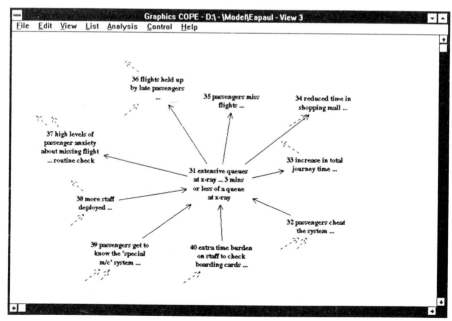

Fig. 5.8 An example of a review display.

Another characteristic of EISs suggested not only by Turban (1988) but also by Harvey and Meiklejohn (1988) is that an EIS should be a 'system tailored to the specific industry in which the company operates and to the specific strategies it has adopted' (Anthony, Dearden and Vancil 1972). COPE achieves this 'tailoring' through its content being comprised of strategies generated from specific theories applying only to that particular organization rather than organizations in general. Furthermore the strategic content has been refined by the executive team thus ensuring that the EIS relates directly to the strategies being pursued by that team.

Additionally COPE through its use of colour and graphics not only adds clarity to the model during the GDSS stage but also fulfils a further feature associated with EIS — that of providing extensive graphic support (Turban 1988, Harvey and Meiklejohn, 1988). Executives are able to use the graphical ability of COPE to view specific information in a variety of ways thus helping them to better understand why they agreed to a particular strategic objective and how to achieve it.

5.3 PREREQUISITES FOR EFFECTIVE GROUP DECISION SUPPORT

Effective group decision support depends upon being able to meet two straightforward necessary but not sufficient conditions. The first is the demand for 'real-time' working thus requiring a very fast response from the software. This in turn ensures that input can be made at close to the speed of commentary of the group, and analyses can be made while the group is working. In practice this means that 'on-the-hoof' analyses must take no longer than about thirty seconds. For the group to be supported effectively it must gain support at the time when the group is thinking, rather than as the result of 'backroom work'. This prerequisite not only depends on the design and demands of the software, but also on the processing speed of the hardware. It is this second condition that has changed in recent years — the processing speed of the 80386 chip and its availability in personal computers that has created new opportunities for 'on-the-hoof' work.

The second important prerequisite for a GDSS is that it should meet the social needs of a working group. The group is actively seeking to reward itself with progress as a workshop continues. It is used to providing this through summaries from the 'chairman', and through an awareness that analytical progress is being made towards a conclusion. Individuals 'finish' with tasks rather than 'solve' them (Eden 1987) which may result in one member finishing with a task before other members of the group. Thus members of the group can become uninterested, feel they have arrived at robust conclusions, and become more interested in another issue before decision support software is ready to perform its analytical purpose. Many decision support software packages demand that the user completes 100% of data entry before any analyses can be undertaken. In GDS it is vital that the group can gain rewards from the decision support system with incomplete data. This means a GDSS should be highly interactive by showing the group that the system is continually providing support.

An additional social need of the group is that 'progress' must be seen to be made and 'added-value' generated. A GDSS should therefore provide the group with a history (Eden 1990d) in a similar way to that which is provided by the use of large sheets of paper progressively filling wall space during 'low-tech' strategy workshops (Friend and Hickling 1987). A group problem-solving activity usually works well when it is fun and entertaining. In GDS this can be expressed by providing a system that makes active use of colourful graphics and so attracts the attention of participants because it is attractive in the way that graphic art can be. A GDS may also provide entertainment through the cross-linkages as members are able to see how new ideas interrelate with previous ideas and begin to understand the views and problems of other members.

When a group is using a GDSS the support system itself is usually designed to facilitate the workshop by providing structure to the discussion. To this extent the GDS is replacing the role of the traditional chairman, and, some would claim, enabling greater democracy (Watson, DeSanctis and Poole 1988) amongst the group. However there is a great danger that the support system focuses too much on the content aspects of group problem solving and too little on the social process of problem solving (Phillips 1990). An important prerequisite of GDSS design is that it balances the social management role of a facilitator and the problem structuring and analytical role of formal model building.

Finally the physical environment of a GDSS needs to be carefully thought through (Eden 1990d Hickling 1990). It is interesting how firm Harvey-Jones is about this topic — 'one area of concern which top management tends to neglect is that of the environment in which discussions are held ... this can have a very substantial effect on the type and quality of the discussion (Harvey-Jones 1988). Hi-tech environments such as the POD (Austin 1987) do not necessarily support a group in positive ways. Our own experience and research with senior management groups suggests that a balance between a hi-tech core which is 'visible' in the sense of providing computer support but as 'invisible' as possible with respect to overall environment is important (Ackermann and Eden 1989).

Most of these prerequisites impact upon the probability of executives making effective use of an Executive Information System as well as their being receptive to a computer-aided GDSS. Those that are especially important are the prerequisites of speed, colour and the lack of reliance on backroom work. The prerequisite of speed lies in the power of the hardware and 'it has only been in the past few years that technology has become sufficiently flexible and powerful to make EIS a practical proposition' (Harvey and Meiklejohn 1988). This speed not only enables the executives to manage the large amounts of information available but also, if they should desire, carry out 'quick analysis' on the information without having to wait for long periods of time. This waiting is coupled with the need to have a system that does not require backroom work. If the executive has to ask for the information to be provided for him, it is likely to arrive later than he needs and may no longer be relevant. Graphics and colour as mentioned earlier are also prerequisites.

5.4   SUCCESS IN GROUP DECISION SUPPORT

Several authors have proposed criteria for the success of group decision support; however Watson, DeSanctis and Poole (1988) have recently delivered a particularly considered view of these criteria based upon their own research. Some of the key elements of these criteria are that:
- more democratic decision making should emerge
- the impact of group members' social approval of one another should be reduced
- ideas should become the object of discussion rather than the proponents of the ideas
- conflict within the group should be reduced
- keyboard effort should not lower group efficiency
- decision quality should be improved
- consensus amongst team members should be higher
- discussion should be more substantial
- the confidence of a group in its decision should be higher
- the problem-solving process used should be transparent to the group
- there should be no increase in the social distance between participants
- the GDSS should be seen as a tool not as a 'group director'
- the group should not become overly concerned with procedural matters.

This list of criteria is not intended to be exhaustive but rather picks out those which seem most interesting in the present context; nevertheless they are all either explicit or implicit in the research evaluation conducted by Watson et al.

Some of these criteria are not necessary to the success of GDS but rather reflect the values of the researchers (Eden 1987b; Ackermann and Eden 1989). For example the notion that democracy is a good thing is a matter for debate; what is more relevant is to consider the way in which the power base of participants changes with computer-based GDS, and the way in which specific factors that are often correlated with democracy change. It may be the wish of the manager buying into the process to ensure that participants feel they have had more 'air time' in order that a greater consensus and commitment occurs, but she may also not demand that this actually happens because she may lose control of the ability to 'mobilize bias' (Schattsneider 1960) and 'manage meaning' (Pettigrew 1977).

Similarly social approval is an important characteristic to study but it is never going to be removed by the imposition of a GDSS, rather it is likely to be changed. Factors such as the skills that participants demonstrate in the use of, for example, keyboards may become significant features in the influence process (Manteii 1988). Such skills are still unlikely to be related to the quality of ideas. Nevertheless some research seems to be indicating that if all members of a group are given the opportunity to participate (actively or passively) in problem solving (through group decision support) then there is less likelihood that participants involve themselves in settling other (hidden) agenda items that will generate dysfunctional social dynamics (Applegate, Konsynski and Nunamaker 1987). The aim with SODA GDS is to maintain participation by demonstrating to those using air time that they have been heard (not just the words but the meaning — collecting concepts or crucial 'chunks' of data and setting them within the context of other concepts) and so release them from the requirement to repeat themselves. If members of a group do not repeat themselves then it is possible for others to 'get a word in edgeways' and/or the meeting time reduced. If a group becomes aware of increased productivity then they develop a more positive attitude to the meeting.

If GDS does provide a more efficient forum then it is likely that the extra air time will mean views expressed will be deeper and more subtle than would have otherwise been the case. It is a common experience of meetings that there is little time to express views that are beyond 'motherhood and apple-pie'. However, the expression and visual record of deeper views inevitably surfaces as more conflict, albeit at a more subtle level, than can occur otherwise. Thus, when COPE and SODA are used as a GDSS, conflict is not necessarily decreased in the first instance. Conflict is allowed to surface rather than remain as the potential for sabotage after the workshop. The GDSS is designed as a structured way to manage conflict towards consensus that is lasting.

Watson et al. have explored the list of success criteria through experiments with student groups working on relatively well-structured problems. Such research is clearly important and useful, whereas the descriptions of work with senior management groups cannot be easily validated, to discover how groups working on highly confidential and very messy issues have responded to a GDSS is a complex research problem. Such research is particularly complicated by the need to recognize and account for the political and social history of the group and the extent to which the group addresses strategic issues in the full knowledge that they have a future together. A student group has no relevant history, no important future together, and can only be expected to work on well-structured problems.

5.5 SUCCESS IN EIS

Paralleling the criteria for success in a GDSS, various EIS authors have suggested various characteristics for increasing the chance for a successful EIS. Turban (1988) proposes that EISs have at least some of the following:

- EIS's principal use is in tracking and control
- it is tailored to the individual executive's decision-making style
- it contains superb graphics capabilities so that information can be presented graphically in several different ways
- it is designed to rapidly produce information for decisions made under pressure
- the system is user friendly; it can be used by the executives themselves
- EIS is designed to fit the corporate culture and style
- it provides status access; namely, rapid access to current information
- EIS filters, compresses and tracks critical data
- implementation of decisions supported by EIS is usually more difficult than of those decisions supported by DSS
- the database is more diversified, including soft data
- EIS deals mainly with the intelligence phase of decision making
- the decisions supported by the EIS are usually top-level, unstructured decisions.

As different organizations require different systems, it may not be possible to include within the EIS all of the above characteristics but they are intended to act as guidelines for developers.

COPE through its hierarchical structure 'provides a logical path of investigation through the data' (Friend 1987) as executives are able to 'drill down' through the model in a variety of ways. This can be carried out individually or with a manager when explaining what actions he/she is responsible for, and their expected outcomes. As the content has originated from a variety of organizational members it is highly qualitative rather than quantitative, supporting both the characteristic regarding 'soft' data as well as clarifying the difference between EIS and Management Information Systems (those systems relating to highly quantitative information).

Alongside Turban's last requirement fits the need for 'strategic scanning capabilities in an EIS, as well as "executive thought support" rather than decision support' (Zmud 1986). COPE enables executives to 'play' with the model, exploring different options, supporting thought, and so act opportunistically (Eden, Ackermann and Timm, 1990) in relation to external events.

Although much of the literature centres around the need to include qualitative information, good graphics and user-friendliness, it has also been suggested that EISs are only just beginning to achieve some of these goals and that there is a long way still to go. The difficulties in getting EISs accepted within the company are largely unresolved and the information needs of executives still need to be explored and better understood before acceptance of EISs by executives is likely. Those EISs that base their information on contributions from members throughout the organization and which help executives in the practical control and implementation of strategy may provide indicators for other EISs to follow.

5.6 CONCLUDING REMARKS

'I believe ... that in deciding where you would like to be, as opposed to where you are probably going to end up, you need a great deal of discussion and a great deal of development of new thinking and new processes. The idea of doing this through the planning department, or through a paper on strategy presented to the board, seems to me to be quite inadequate. This process involves large amounts of time and constant discussion with those involved lower down the line who will actually execute the strategies on which the whole picture relies. This sort of circular debate, frequently widening out to involve others within and without the company, goes on until all are satisfied that the result is as good as they are going to get.' Harvey-Jones, 1988.

Computer-aided group decision support systems must be able to support this activity as it continues and yet also provide an effective 'transitional object' (De Geus 1988) or 'organizational memory' that carries forward the essence of the discussions. While the SODA method and COPE software aim to do this they are only the beginning of a revolution in the use of computers for helping groups and individuals think creatively — 'such models have exhausted empiricism and placed no bounds on rationality' (Rohrbaugh 1988).

REFERENCES

Ackermann, F. (1990) The role of computers in group decision support, in C. Eden and J. Radford (eds), *Tackling Strategic Problems: The Role of Group Decision Support.* Sage: London.

Ackermann, F. and Eden, C. (1989) Issues in computer and non-computer supported GDSS's. Paper presented to the Operational Research Society Conference, Southampton, September.

Anthony, R.N., Dearden, J. and Vancil, R.F. (1972) Key economic variables, *Management Controls System.* Irwin: Homewood, Ill.

Applegate, L.M., Konsynski, B.R. and Nunamaker, J.F. (1987) A group decision support systems for idea generation and issue analysis in organizational planning, *Journal of Management Information Systems,* 3, 5-19.

Argyris, C. (1983) Action science and intervention, *Journal of Applied Behavioural Science,* 19, 115-140.

Austin, N.C. (1987) A management support environment, *ICL Technical Bulletin,* International Computers: Oxford.

Backoff, R.W. and Nutt, P.C. (1988) A process for strategic management with specific application for the nonprofit organization, in J.M. Bryson and R.C. Einsweiler (eds), *Strategic Planning: Threats and Opportunities for Planners.* Planners Press: Chicago.

Bartunek, J.M. and Moch, M.K. (1987) First-order, second-order, and third-order change and organization development interventions: a cognitive approach, *Journal of Applied Behavioural Science,* 23, 483-500.

Burkan, W.C. (1988) Making EIS work, *Decision Support Systems 1988 Transactions,* 121-136.

Cropper, S., Eden, C. and Ackermann, F. (1990) Keeping sense of accounts using computer-based cognitive maps, *Social Science Computer Review,* 8, 345-366.

De Geus, A. (1988) Planning as learning, *Harvard Business Review,* April-March.

Delbecq, A.L., Van de Ven, A.H. and Gustafson, D.H. (1975) *Group Techniques for Program Planning.* Scott Foreman: Glenview, Ill.

Eden, C. (1987a). Problem solving or problem finishing? in M.C. Jackson and P. Keys (eds), *New Directions in Management Science.* Gower: Aldershot.

Eden, C. (1987b) A response to Watson, DeSanctis and Poole, Personal communication with Marshall Scott Poole, November and January.

Eden, C. (1988) Cognitive mapping: a review, *European Journal of Operational Research,* 36, 1-13.

Eden, C. (1989) Strategic options development and analysis – SODA, in J. Rosenhead (ed.), *Rational Analysis in a Problematic World,* Wiley: London.

Eden, C. (1989a) Operational research as negotiation, in M. Jackson, P. Keys and S. Cropper (eds), *Operational Research and the Social Sciences,* Plenum: New York.

Eden, C. (1990a) Strategic thinking with computers, *Long Range Planning,* in press.

Eden, C. (1990b) Cognitive maps as a visionary tool: strategy embedded in issue management, in R.G. Dyson (ed.), *Strategic Planning: Models and Analytical Techniques,* Wiley: London.

Eden, C. (1990c) The unfolding nature of group decision support – two dimensions of skill, in C. Eden and J. Radford (eds), *Tackling Strategic Problems: The Role of Group Decision Support,* Sage: London.

Eden, C. (1990d) Managing the environment as a means to managing complexity, in C. Eden and J. Radford (eds), *Tackling Strategic Problems: The Role of Group Decision Support,* Sage: London.

Eden, C., Ackermann, F. and Timm, S. (1990) Strategy performance and the performance of strategy, Proceedings of the British Academy of Management Conference, Glasgow, September.

Eden, C., Cropper, S. and Train, C. (1990) Performance and coherence: the strategy review process, Paper presented to Strategic Planning Society, February.

Eden, C., Jones, S. and Sims, D. (1983) *Messing about in Problems,* Pergamon: Oxford.

Friend, D. (1987) The three pillars of an EIS, source unknown.

Friend, J. and Hickling, A. (1987) *Planning under Pressure.* Pergamon: Oxford.

Goold, M. and Quinn, J.J. (1990) The paradox of strategic controls, *Strategic Management Journal,* 11, 43-57.

Harvey-Jones, J. (1988) *Making it Happen.* Collins: London.

Harvey, D. and Meiklejohn, I. (1988) *The Executive Information Systems Report.* Business Intelligence Ltd: London.

Hickling, A. (1990) 'Decision Spaces': a scenario about designing appropriate rooms for group decision management, in C. Eden and J.

Radford (eds), *Tackling Strategic Problems: The Role of Group Decision Support.*, Sage: London.

Manteii, M.M. (1988) Capturing the capture lab concepts: a case study in the design of computer supported meeting environments. Research Paper No. 030988 Centre for Machine Intelligence, Electronic Data Systems Corporation.

Pettigrew, A. (1977) Strategy formulation as a political process, *International Studies in Management and Organization,* 7, 78-87.

Phillips, L. (1990) Decision analysis for group decision support, in C. Eden and J. Radford (eds), *Tackling Strategic Problems: The Role of Group Decision Support.* Sage: London.

Phillips, L. (1990) On facilitating groups. Paper presented to ESRC Seminar No. 1 — Operational Research and the Social Sciences, London, October.

Pizey, H. and Huxham, C. (1990) 1990 and beyond: developing a process for group decision support in large scale event planning, *European Journal of Operational Research,* forthcoming.

Rockart, J.F. (1979) Chief executives define their own data needs, *Harvard Business Review*, March-April, 81-92.

Rohrbaugh, J. (1987) Presented to the International Symposium on Future Directions in Strategic Management, Toronto, September.

Schattsneider, E.E. (1960) *The Semi-Sovereign People,* Holt, Reinhart and Winston: New York.

Spender, J.C. (1989) *Industry Recipes, and Enquiry into the Nature and Sources of Managerial Judgement,* Basil Blackwell: Oxford.

Telford, W.A., Ackermann, F. and Cropper, S. (1990) Managing Quality, in R. O'Moore, S. Bengtsson, J.R. Bryant and J.S. Bryden (eds), *Medical Informatics Europe '90 — Proceedings,* Glasgow, August.

Turban, E. (1988) *Decision Support and Expert Systems — Managerial Perspectives,* Macmillan: New York.

Watson, R., DeSanctis, G. and Poole, M.S. (1988) Using a GDSS to facilitate group consensus: some intended and unintended consequences, *MIS Quarterly,* forthcoming.

Zmud, R. (1986) Supporting senior executives through decision support technologies: a review and directions for future research, *Decision Support Systems: A Decade in Perspective,* Elsevier Science Publishers: North-Holland.

6 Gaining corporate commitment to change

L. Phillips
Decision Analysis Unit, London School of Economics and Political Science

6.1 INTRODUCTION

For many years I have worked with managing directors and senior executives who want to sort out messy and complex issues involving change in their organizations: strategic management, organization structure, resource allocation, policy making, and others. Although each organization recognizes that its problems are unique, I have noticed that some issues are common to almost everyone. It is these that I would like to present in this paper, along with some lessons derived from project work with these organizations. My hope is that some of these observations will be relevant to your own organizations, and suggest ways of dealing more effectively with serious issues that are the special province of managing directors and senior executives.

6.2 SEVEN ISSUES

In reflecting on my experiences with different organizations, I find that seven issues emerge as common to many senior people. I'm sure there are more, but these seven have the special quality that they cannot be given answers that are right or wrong, nor can they be ignored without consequence. They are 'messy' issues that matter.

6.2.1 Differences in perspective

'If only he weren't so bloody minded!' Often felt, rarely uttered, but a frequently perceived roadblock to progress. The finance director who stresses the bottom-line monetary consequences, the personnel director who is concerned about the effect of decisions on employee morale or on the unions, the marketing manager worried about market share, the research director who pushes new ventures, each contributes a perspective that admits to a different resolution of the issues.

In a meeting with an insurance company that was developing a plan for a new market, considerable disagreement arose amongst the directors about whether the company should get into this market. At a break, the senior actuary, a Scotsman, took me aside. 'The trouble with this company,' he said, rolling his r's, 'is that the other directors don't know how to run the business. Now in Scotland we do it right; actuaries run the business!' The need is clear: to develop a shared perspective on the issues at hand. This shared perspective needs to legitimize the individual views of the other executives, yet it should somehow be bigger than any of them, and resolve the individual differences.

6.2.2   The corporate collegium

Closely related to the need for a shared perspective is the way directors of an organization work together. Unlike lower levels, where the relationship is that of manager-to-subordinate, directors of a company work in collegial fashion. Decisions are made by consensus, and the mode of working is one of collaboration and consultation.

But this can give rise to problems when the directors do not share a sense of common purpose, and when differences in perspectives give rise to divergent solutions to problems.

The managing director and general managers of a food company were holding their annual meeting to revise the five-year plan. At the end of the first day a plan had been proposed that met with the approval of the general managers; it was a plan that essentially said to stick to the knitting and do what we have always done well. The managing director was concerned that no place had been found to introduce new products. The next day, a longer time horizon was considered, up to ten years, and then new products looked attractive, but only by reducing the spend on some existing products. The managing director was well pleased: 'This is the first plan we have developed that I can fully sign on to.' But some of the general managers were not looking so happy.

Particularly at board level, directors need to pull together. This is often possible only when they share a sense of common purpose, and that's not always easy to come by.

6.2.3 Making it happen

Even if perspectives are shared and a sense of common purpose has developed amongst the senior executives, they often find it difficult to 'make it happen'. 'These people are not facing the facts,' one general manager complained. 'If they did, they would do what I have suggested.' The temptation is to provide more and better information, to develop ever bigger and more comprehensive management information systems, for when everyone has sufficient data, then decision making will be easy.

The problem with this argument is that it equates decision making with the provision of information. Decision theory (Hogarth 1987) makes it clear that while information is one important ingredient to good decisions, there is another, equally-important ingredient: value judgements.

A computer company was reorganized into profit centres with transfer prices governed by the actual price at the time of sale, an arrangement that was intended to motivate the sales outlets. One sales centre found that it could increase the chance of selling computer systems by bundling in software for free. This resulted in a zero transfer price for the profit centre that produced the software, and soon their profit-and-loss statement was looking very sorry indeed. The sales outlet started to experience difficulty in obtaining software from that profit centre.

The sales centre's decision to give away software, and the software centre's decision to hold back in providing the software were governed by value judgements, by what was in the best interests of the group. No amount of additional information could resolve the conflict.

It is obvious that two people with the same information might decide differently; otherwise, we would all buy the same car! These differences are attributable to value judgements: how good a particular car is in certain respects, how important its features are to us, and the extent to which we are willing to trade off the features, like cost against better performance. The MD mentioned in the previous section valued the long term more than the short term, but it was the other way around for the general managers. Additional information wouldn't have resolved their conflict in value judgements.

Thus, to 'make it happen', it is necessary to integrate information with values. Usually this is done in the head of the decision maker; information is obtained, value judgements made, and then action follows. Facing the facts is not sufficient to 'make it happen'. Somehow, values must also be communicated and shared.

6.2.4 Planning in the face of uncertainty

Many senior executives act as though the future is completely under their control. Of course unexpected things happen, they acknowledge, but if you have a clear vision of the future, then you can steer the organization around the obstacles. There's some truth to this; creating the future is part of the job of the managing director. But that is best done by acknowledging uncertainty, not by pretending it doesn't exist.

The development division of one company was preparing for a seven-fold growth in the business over the next five years. Resources for the growth were to come from the company's profits, most of which were attributable to a single, highly successful product. Strategies were agreed for this growth, and new facilities and equipment were acquired to accommodate the development of new products that would create the growth. Without warning, a new, cheaper, more effective product appeared on the market in competition with this company's major product. Within weeks, a strategy of growth had to be changed to one of contraction, but too much had already been committed. The company was taken over.

Once a company is embarked on a course of action, it is often difficult to make a substantial qualitative shift on any of the key business drivers, though this is usually required for real progress to be made. Instead, planning is done by offering incremental changes on last year, so the only thing senior executives can do is approve minor twiddles.

The need is for senior executives to identify the key business drivers, then agree and implement a qualitative shift in strategy on one or more of them, taking account of uncertainties about the future. In short, to manage strategically.

6.2.5 Hard versus soft objectives

In choosing strategies, senior executives are often painfully aware that no strategy meets all the organization's objectives. An example is the conflict often experienced between short-term profit and long-term potential, e.g., some cash cows, if milked too often, dry up. But other conflicts can also arise: some profit may have to be forgone to prevent environmental harm, to reduce risk, to improve employee morale or to increase the safety of plant operation.

Recent research at the LSE's Decision Analysis Unit looked at the balance of weight managers and executives place on 'hard' and 'soft' objectives in determining strategies. Profit, market share and revenue were classed as 'hard' objectives, while 'soft' objectives included future potential, risk reduction, company image and employee morale. The research showed that middle-level managers place more weight on hard than soft objectives, but for senior executives it's the other way around. They don't ignore the hard objectives, but they are more concerned about the soft ones.

Although the research has not yet identified why this is so, or if it is generally true outside the few groups that were studied, it seems plausible that the longer time horizons considered by top managers require them to focus on the soft objectives. Perhaps hard results are obtained by getting things right on the soft objectives.

Whatever the explanation, there is a clear need in determining effective strategies to find the right balance amongst conflicting objectives.

6.2.6 The 'commons dilemma'

Conflict arises in every large organization between managers who compete to gain a bigger slice of the 'pie'. When an organization is growing, this is not a serious problem; budgets can be increased every year. But when growth is limited, restructuring is occurring, opportunities are limited, or crises are arising, each manager may withdraw to become a 'king of the castle', preferring to be left alone to optimize the use of his or her own resources. Teamwork disappears, and even if each manager is using the available resource optimally, the boss can see that the collective result is not optimal. Seven eastern European sales outlets for a multi-national company had been given growth targets by the European division of the company. Country managers were operating independently, responding to local conditions, and making the best use they could of the resources available to them. Although opportunities were infinite, resources were limited, and they had been unable to achieve any substantial growth. When a new territory manager called them together to examine and evaluate their strategies, it was discovered that the sum of the individual strategies was far from the collective best: every manager was following the wrong strategy.

This may seem paradoxical; if each person is doing his or her best, why isn't the sum of these efforts a collective best? The answer is that they would be if opportunities and threats were identical from one manager to the next. But when one manager's opportunities are greater than another's, then a collective best can be achieved by taking resource from the manager with lesser opportunity and giving it to the manager with greater opportunity. The benefit lost by one will be more than made up by the other.

This phenomenon is so ubiquitous that it has been given a name: the commons dilemma. This refers to the overgrazing of the 'common land' by sheep and cattle that occurred in fourteenth-century England. It was in each herder's interests to add more stock because the cost in grazing land was more than offset by the individual herder's increment of profit, but of course the collective result became worse.

One solution is to centralize all allocation of resource, as has occurred in many socialist countries. When this happens in an organization, it can restore the efficient use of resources, but then individual managers may lose their sense of ownership of the work as resource constraints are imposed from above. A better approach, one which provides both a sense of ownership of the work and a collective best use of the available resource, is to require managers competing for their slices of the pie to discuss and agree amongst themselves, in light of their differing opportunities and threats, the allocation of resource that will provide a collectively preferred solution. In short, the need is for managers to face up to the tradeoffs that exist between their areas of responsibility.

6.2.7 Decision taking

I could have subsumed all of the above under the general need for better decisions in organizations. Had I done so, you would probably have ignored me, for I have yet to meet a manager or executive who will admit in public that his or her decisions could be improved. We may complain about our memories, but never about our decisions. John Adair, in reporting the results of a 1976 survey of executives in industry and commerce (Adair 1985), notes that the first-ranked attribute of value at the top level of management was the ability to take decisions. Ed Mahler, a senior executive at DuPont has estimated that roughly 100,000 decisions had to be taken before the wristwatch on your wrist could be delivered as a finished product. He asks, 'Could all of those decisions have been good ones?' The research literature on decision-making answers that question with a firm 'no'. Thirty years of research on people's judgements and decisions shows that we make mistakes, usually without knowing it (Dawes 1988). Much of life is like playing poker without ever finding out what cards were in the hands of the other players; when business is like that, it is no wonder that we make poor decisions and don't discover how bad they were.

Head office told the managing director of one of its operating companies that much more money was being spent on TV advertising in that country than in any other country. The MD felt that the expenditure was necessary, for they were creating the market in that country, whereas it was already established in others. To provide a reply to head office, he and his executives gathered to argue the pros and cons of spending so much. Although the pros outweighed the cons, in their view, they did not feel that head office would be persuaded. Instead, it looked as though they would have to reduce advertising in one part of the country and measure the effect, a potentially expensive exercise, especially if they were correct.

Many executives decide about an option by considering its pros and cons: if the pros outweigh the cons, the option is accepted, otherwise it is rejected. I've named this the single option fallacy. Why is it a fallacy? Because the alternative is not considered. Rejecting an option requires accepting the alternative, even if it is the status quo. And unless the pros and cons of the alternative are also considered, rejecting an option might lead one to accept an alternative whose cons outweigh the pros even more. It's no use discovering that one is in the frying pan and so, without looking first, jumping into the fire!

Some years ago, the Ford Motor Company conducted a cost-benefit analysis of the option to relocate the petrol tank in the Ford Pinto car. The cost of relocating it to a safer position was compared to the benefits in terms of lives saved, injuries prevented and vehicles saved. The costs were found to be greater than the benefits, so the petrol tank was not moved. If an analysis had also been made of the alternative, not moving the tank, Ford might have anticipated the numerous lawsuits that led to cases in more than 50 courts, with millions of dollars of damages awarded, all amongst a flurry of adverse publicity.

Many more fallacies of judgement and decision-taking are documented in the books by Adair, Dawes and Hogarth. At last count, I identified over thirty kinds of error that people make in both everyday and business situations. Clearly, there is a need to improve decision taking, especially since it is the quality senior executives consider to be the most crucial.

6.2.8 Summary

Work with a variety of organizations has led me to identify seven needs at the level of top management. Executives need to develop a shared perspective on the key issues that concern their organization, and they need a sense of common purpose, for only then will everyone pull together effectively in the same direction. To 'make it happen', it is necessary to integrate information with values, while taking account of uncertainties about the future; this is what is required to manage strategically.

Effective strategies find the right balance amongst conflicting objectives, and they result in collectively best solutions when managers face up to the tradeoffs that exist between their areas of responsibility. Overall, there is a need to improve decision taking in organizations.

6.3   DECISION CONFERENCING IN ACTION

Well, yes, you say, but how can all this happen? There isn't any one way. However, the past two decades have seen the development of a remarkable technology that attempts to improve decision making without regard for the actual content of the decision. This technology, called decision analysis (Watson and Buede 1987), is based on the simple assumption that people often are trying to be coherent in taking decisions within a particular domain. Starting with that innocuous assumption, an entire theory has arisen, a theory which can be applied to any decision, whatever the topic, much like mathematics can be used for many different purposes.

By itself, the technology of decision analysis is not sufficient to resolve the seven issues highlighted in the previous sections. More is needed: an understanding of how individuals form judgements and take decisions, of how groups can enhance or dissipate the creative potential of individuals, and how information technology can provide tools to improve individual and group effectiveness.

6.3.1   Decision conferencing

We have brought these elements together at the LSE in a process known as decision conferencing. This is a two-day session attended by a group of people who attempt to resolve important issues of concern to their organization with the help of a facilitator and some computer modelling. Work is carried out in a group setting to allow the interchange of differing perspectives on the issues. This is encouraged by the facilitator, who attends to group processes but does not contribute to the content of discussions.

Decision analysis provides a variety of structures for modelling the differing perspectives on the issues. The model constructed is not a financial model, or a model of the environment, but a model of participants' judgements: the options they face, the (possibly conflicting) objectives they are trying to meet, their evaluations of the consequences of following the options, and the uncertainty they feel about events that influence the consequences. Information and value judgements are integrated in these models, whose results usually reveal new, higher-level perspectives on the issues.

The results don't come immediately. Initial model results are usually rejected by the group, and these discrepancies between intuition and the model are explored. Sometimes the model is found to be inadequate, and changes are made, but at other times intuitions are revised as the model provides new insights about the issues. Eventually this process of change stabilizes, and remaining differences of opinion are tested in the model to see their effect on the ordering of options. Usually these differences have little influence, so participants can agree about what to do even though there may be no consensus on many of the issues. Thus, the process produces a shared understanding of the issues, though not necessarily agreement about them, and a commitment to action. Most importantly, a sense of common purpose is generated.

A better idea of what decision conferencing can do is shown in Table 6.1. There I have summarized, for each of five real cases, the business need and the obstacles to attaining the goal; these led some key players to decide that a decision conference might be an appropriate way of resolving the difficulties. In addition, I have described briefly how decision conferencing helped.

Two of these cases (the one on resolving conflict and the one that considered a territorial marketing strategy), will be elaborated in the next sections to give a better idea of the variety of ways that a decision conference can help.

6.3.2 Business strategy

An extremely successful new business initiative needed more investment, but managers were divided on how that should be achieved. One group felt that the strategy started two years earlier should be completed, enabling the company to maintain ownership and control. Another group argued that future growth should be funded by selling off part of the business initiative.

After some discussion, six options were identified: pull out, sell off, sell 75%, partnership, current plan and sell 75% plus focus. These options were different from one another, in ways that mattered, on both financial and non-financial objectives, as shown in Figure 6.1. The options were then assessed for their relative desirability on each of the bottom-level criteria, and the criteria were weighted to reflect their relative importance.

Table 6.1 Decision conference cases

The need	Obstacles	How decision conferencing helped
To develop a five-year plan.	Company directors could not agree key elements of strategy.	Differences about the relative importance of long-term growth compared to short-term profit were found to be the cause of Directors' disagreements. These were resolved and actions agreed about products, including new ones.
To design a production facility for an innovative product.	The design team disagreed about how to scale up this new process.	The manufacturing process was broken down into a series of stages, and various group techniques were used to obtain agreement about the design at each stage. The resulting plans were subsequently approved without change.
To resolve conflict between two groups.	Designers of a new product needed more resource but managers were unwilling to commit more money.	The judgements of these two groups were combined in a single computer model that enabled participants to develop and test several new options. These enabled both groups to achieve their objectives. The company adopted one option which involved a joint venture and partial sell-off.
To allocate an advertising budget.	Brand managers each wanted more resource, which in total exceeded the budget.	The managers generated several advertising strategies, at different levels of resource, for each brand. Tradeoffs between the brands were judged by the group, and a computer model looked at all possible combinations of strategies. The one agreed by the group gave some managers more resource and some less.
To re-consider a territorial marketing strategy.	Marketing strategies in the seven countries of a territory were not achieving growth targets.	The territory manager met with his country managers to consider alternative strategies for each country. Computer modelling enabled territory strategies to be compared, and revealed that managers were following the wrong strategies in every country. A new strategy, involving cutbacks in some countries, was agreed and implemented. Revenues and profits subsequently doubled.

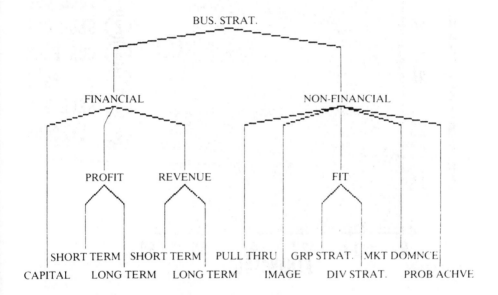

Fig. 6.1 Value tree for the business strategy problem.

Taking a weighted average of all the assessments gave the result shown in Figure 6.2. Option 1, pull out, is obviously bad on both financial and non-financial criteria. The current plan, option 3, is fairly good on the non-financial criteria, but is less good under financial considerations. Surprisingly, selling 75%, option 5, is reasonably good on both clusters of criteria.

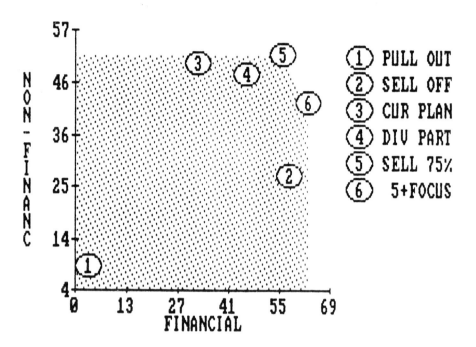

Fig. 6.2 Overall result on the financial and non-financial criteria for the six options.

The model facilitated examination of the strengths and weaknesses of each option, and enabled the group to compare options, like 5 and 6, which lie on the outside border. During these analyses, the two opposing groups began to change their views, and started to generate new options. First, they considered adding intensive marketing to the 75% sell-off, then a joint venture, and finally a combination of selling 75% with a joint venture. The results of this revised model are shown in Figure 6.3.

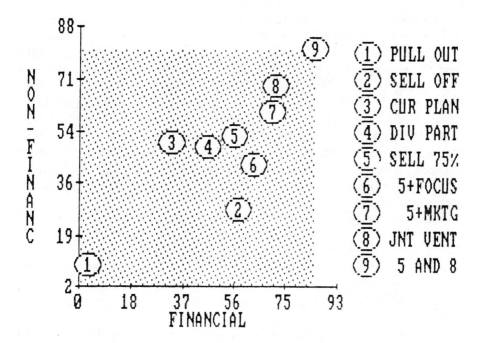

Fig. 6.3 The final result in the business strategy problem.

Note that the three new strategies are all better than the original ones. Thus, the decision conference helped the group to be more constructive and creative, with the result that all participants agreed a precise strategic direction that involved both a partial sell-off and a joint venture. That has now come to fruition, to the financial (and non-financial) benefit of the company. Two months after the event, a senior participant commented 'It was the turning point for our group. It changed the mindset of our management team in a very constructive way and we are now following the new strategy very closely.'

6.3.3   Territorial marketing strategy

This case concerns a sales management team that was operating in seven eastern European countries. Although each country manager had adopted a strategy that made the most of the limited resource available to him, growth had eluded the team. The country manager felt that it was worth reconsidering the strategies being pursued by his country managers, so he called them together for a decision conference.

The session began with each manager describing his current strategy and the resource he had available. Each manager was then invited to prepare alternative plans, some requiring more, and some less, resource than the current plan for the next three years. Since the overall objective of the territory was to grow profitably at no increase in risk, the alternative plans for each country were evaluated by the group on criteria of profit, revenue growth, risk and future potential (the potential at the end of three years for generating profit and revenue in the next three years). Opportunities and threats in each country were considered so that tradeoffs between countries could be assessed in the form of weights. In addition, weights reflecting the relative importance of the criteria were judged by the group.

A computer model was used to evaluate all possible combinations of country strategies (105,000 possibilities altogether!). The result is shown in Figure 6.4. All 105,000 combinations are either on the curve or below it; there are no low-cost, high-benefit strategies. One combination, the current strategy in every country, is shown at point P. Also shown are a better, B, and a cheaper, C, plan. That is to say, the current plan can be substantially improved.

How the improvements should be made are shown in Table 6.2. The levels shown by the boxes in each row represent the different strategies considered by that country; the box containing the 'P' represents the current strategy, while lower-numbered boxes stand for cheaper strategies, and higher-numbered boxes more expensive strategies. The table shows how the current plan, P, should be changed to be better, B, or cheaper, C. Thus, to achieve more benefit at no increase in cost, cutbacks should be made in Greece, the USSR and Bulgaria, with the resource that releases being given to the other four countries. Because the 'P' stands alone in every box, managers were following the wrong strategy in every country. The country managers then realized that the best possible plan, B, for the territory as a whole was not the sum of the individual country plans, P. The decision conference showed how the commons dilemma could be resolved.

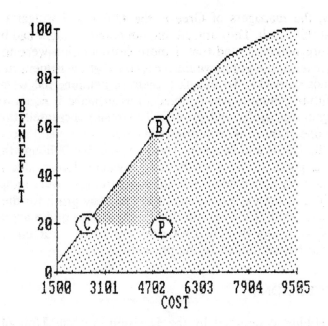

Fig. 6.4 The current plan, P, compared to a better, B, and a cheaper, C, plan.

Table 6.2 How the current plan could be improved to a better, B, or a cheaper, C, plan.

VARIABLE	LEVEL						
	1	2	3	4	5	6	7
1 GREECE	CB	P					
2 YUGOSLAVIA	C		P		B		
3 USSR	CB	P					
4 POLAND		P		CB			
5 CSSR	C	P	B				
6 HUNGARY		P	CB				
7 BULGARIA	CB	P					

Initially, the managers of Greece, the USSR and Bulgaria were not happy about this result. They argued that not enough weight had been given to their future potential, and that if more consideration were to be given to the longer term, the group would recognize that investment in them was desirable, not cutbacks. To examine their contention, the weight in the model on future potential was doubled so as to make it equal to the sum of the weights on profit and growth. The result increased the level of spending in one of the other countries, but cutbacks were still recommended in Greece, the USSR and Bulgaria. They realized that although their future potential was good, it was even better elsewhere. Eventually, the group agreed to cutbacks in two countries, and new strategies were adopted in all the others. The result was a doubling in revenue and profit for the territory. As the Director said: 'I am certain that the directions and plans we agreed during those two days in May 1984 were the reasons for our success in 1985.' Growth has continued to the present day.

6.4   CONCLUSIONS

Follow-up studies conducted by the Decision Analysis Unit of decision conferences held in this country and the United States, for organizations in both the private and public sectors, consistently receive higher ratings from participants than traditional meetings. Organizations using decision conferencing report that the process helps them to arrive at better and more acceptable solutions than they can achieve using their usual procedures, and agreement is reached much more quickly. Many decision conferences have broken through stalemates created previously by lack of consensus, by the complexity of the problem, by vagueness and conflict of objectives, and by failure to think creatively and freshly about the problem. Decision conferencing lends structure to thinking, and allows all perspectives on the issues to be represented. The process takes the heat out of disagreements and facilitates communication amongst participants. Assumptions are surfaced, creative thinking encouraged, and commitment is built. Overall, decision conferencing builds a sense of common purpose. And the tangible output is very practical: a list of conclusions and key issues, and an action plan that indicates who is to do what by when.

Experience suggests that decision conferencing works best in organizations when four conditions are met reasonably well. First, time allowing, consultation should typically precede decision making. The participative style of decision conferencing can be adapted to a variety of leadership styles, but is sometimes resisted by authoritarian executives. Second, communication links should exist across the organization's divisions and sub-divisions, so that information flows laterally as well as vertically,

This helps to ensure that the information needed in a decision conference will be available. Third, a climate of problem solving should exist in the organization, so that options can be freely explored. If the organization's style encourages the manipulation of options to serve predetermined solutions, then decision conferencing will be resisted because new, un-anticipated solutions may emerge. Finally, authority and accountability should be well-distributed throughout the organization, neither concentrated at the top nor totally distributed toward the bottom. This ensures that participants hold the authority to carry out the action plan that they create.

I hope that I have managed to communicate one approach to resolving some difficult issues faced by most senior managers and executives. It is through structured work in groups that participants can exchange perspectives on difficult issues, develop a sense of common purpose, integrate information with values, develop effective strategies that take account of uncertainty and balance conflicting objectives while considering tradeoffs. The result should be better decisions.

Let me conclude with some observations on why decision conferencing helps participants to gain commitment to corporate change. First, participants are selected so as to represent all key perspectives on the issues, with the result that agreed actions are unlikely to be stopped by someone else arguing that the group failed to consider a major factor. Second, with no fixed agenda or prepared presentations, the meeting becomes 'live', the group works in the 'here-and-now', and participants get to grips with the deeper issues that help to build consensus.

Third, the model plays a crucial role in generating commitment. All model inputs are generated by the participants and nothing is imposed, so that the final model is the creation of the group. The model is 'owned' by the group, so its results are accepted, and participants buy in to the consequent action plan. In addition, the model allows the consequences of differences of opinion to be explored in ways that are inaccessible to words. Usually, the results are hardly affected by these differences, and when they are, substantial areas of agreement remain. The importance of this feature cannot be overemphasized, for the model permits individual judgements to differ even though agreement has been reached about actions. Thus, each participant can preserve aspects of his or her individuality, while still committing to the collective best solution agreed by the group. Many groups fail because the inevitable conflict between individual identity and the group life is not managed with the result that destructive forces dominate the group and effective work cannot be accomplished without rigid controls that stifle dissent and creativity.

Fourth, information technology permits instant playback of model results, and allows the results of changes to be seen immediately. The computer never intrudes, and is subservient to the process of clarifying the issues. Participants can try out ideas, without commitment, on the model, then develop and refine their views as insights about the issues are generated. This happens to all participants, with the result that they come to a shared understanding of the issues.

Finally, the environment in which the group works is carefully arranged to ensure that the group is maximally effective. Surprisingly, most work rooms don't facilitate productive work. Long, rectangular tables prevent easy eye-to-eye contact and reinforce status differences; insufficient, inadequate and poorly-lit boards and flip-charts prevent easy sharing of information; overhead projectors or other audio-visual equipment usually has to be arranged beforehand, with the result that it isn't. Paper shuffling becomes the order of the day.

New research at the University of Arizona shows that with properly designed work rooms, productivity gains of 100% can be obtained. This is an astonishing figure, but it is confirmed by observations of people working in the LSE Pod. (The Pod is an octagonally-shaped room that seats up to twelve people around a circular table, and makes available, unobtrusively, a variety of computers and audio-visual equipment.) Thus, the working environment is a crucial ingredient in helping to achieve group commitment.

None of these features is, by itself, unique. What is new is their combination, with the result that the whole seems to be substantially more than the sum of its parts. We are only beginning to understand why this is so, but it is clear that new ways of working are emerging. We are discovering ways to enhance the capabilities of individuals, and to release the creative potential of groups in ways that enable both the individual and the organization to benefit.

REFERENCES

Adair, J. (1985) *Effective Decision Making,* London: Pan Books.

Dawes, R. (1988) *Rational Choice in an Uncertain World,* San Diego: Harcourt Brace Jovanovich.

Hogarth, R. M. (1987) *Judgment and Choice: The Psychology of Decision,* 2nd edn, Chichester: Wiley.

Watson, S. and Buede, D. (1987) *Decision Synthesis: The Principles and Practice of Decision Analysis,* Cambridge: Cambridge University Press.

Part Four

Supporting Multi-criteria Decisions

7 The role of sensitivity analysis in decision analysis

S. French
School of Computer Studies, University of Leeds

7.1 INTRODUCTION

Throughout engineering, management science and operational research, there is a recognized need to conduct a sensitivity analysis on any calculations. How robust are the results to small changes in the input data? Decision analysis has many quantitative aspects. Thus sensitivity analysis must play a role in any decision analysis. However, there are many differences of emphasis in applying sensitivity analysis to the calculations within a decision analysis compared with, say, its application to the stress calculations on a load-bearing beam in an engineering project. In this paper we will explore those differences: but first we need to embark on some simple context-setting, showing what styles of sensitivity analysis are or will shortly become possible in additive value calculations. Later we turn to a discussion of the role, or rather roles, that sensitivity analysis can and should fulfil. Additive value techniques are far from the only decision analytic techniques; so we broaden our discussion to include subjective probability and expected multi-attribute utility calculations. We close by introducing a general framework for sensitivity analysis in decision analytic calculations.

7.2 DECISION ANALYSIS USING ADDITIVE VALUE FUNCTIONS

One of the most common decision analytic techniques is the evaluation of alternatives by means of additive value functions. Those interested in the theory of these may consult the literature [DYE79], [FRE86, Chapter 4], [KEE76, Chapter 3], [WIN86, Chapters 8 and 9]. Here it will be sufficient to rely, by and large, on intuition.

A value function v(.) represents a decision maker's[1] (DM's) preferences between alternatives in the following sense. For any pair of alternatives, a and b:

---

1 Initially we shall refer to the decision maker in the singular. We address issues which arise when groups of decision makers are responsible for a decision later in the paper.

$$v(a) \geq v(b) \tag{1}$$

if and only if he[2] holds a to be at least as good as b. If he strictly prefers a to b, then strict inequality holds in (WEAK REP). Thus v(.) assigns a higher number to the more preferred alternative.

Suppose that the alternatives in the decision problem are represented according to their levels on a number of attributes. For instance, in a problem relating to the installation of a new computer system the attributes might be: installation costs; conversion costs of software, databases, etc.; running costs; performance (MIPS); memory (Mb); diskspace (Gb); disk access times (μsecs); stability of supplier; and reliability of hardware (mtbf). (NB. In a real problem rather more attributes might be specified, but these will serve for illustration.) Thus each possible computer system would be described by a vector of attribute levels:

$$\text{comp\_sys} = (\text{inst\_cost, conv\_cost, run\_cost, perf, mem, disk\_sp,}$$
$$\text{disk\_acc, stab, hard\_rel,}). \tag{2}$$

Thus a particular alternative might be:

HAL = (£1m, 0.8m, 0.5m, 25MIPs, 64Mb, 5.4Gb, 5μsecs, 70, 27days)

Note the attribute score of 70 for HAL on stab, the stability of supplier. There being no objective scale of measurement for such a quality, this would be a subjective assessment by the DM. We will return to such assessments shortly.

The set of attributes used in a problem are usually grouped together in a hierarchy. Figure 7.1 shows a possible hierarchy for this example. The hierarchy groups together the attributes in ways that:

• are suggestive cognitively and, therefore, helpful to the DM's understanding
• help structure and subsequent sensitivity analysis.

---

2   Masculine pronouns, etc. are used throughout to represent persons of either gender.

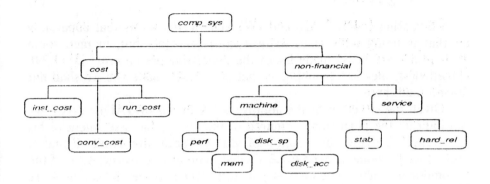

Fig. 7.1 An example of an attribute hierarchy.

The first point should be clear intuitively; we illustrate the latter point shortly.

Henceforth, we shall assume that all alternatives in a decision problem are represented as vectors of k attribute levels, writing alternatives as:

$$a = (a_1, a_2, \ldots, a_k),$$

where a_i is the level achieved by alternative a on the ith attribute.

In many cases the value function $v(.)$ is a 'nice' function of these levels. In particular, $v(.)$ often can be shown to have an additive form:

$$v(a) = v_1(a_1) + v_2(a_2) + \ldots + v_k(a_k)$$
$$= \sum i \, v_i(a_i). \tag{3}$$

Discussions of the circumstances in which additivity holds may be found in the literature: [DYE79], [FRE86], [KEE76], [WIN86]. In fact, there is an element of chicken and egg in all such discussions since the choice of attributes is closely entwined with the validity of an additive representation. The folklore among many decision analysts is that it is usually possible to select appropriate attributes in a problem such that additivity holds.

A variation on the additive form (ADD VAL) is usually adopted in practice. As given the component value functions $v_i(.)$ are all assessed on the same scale. There are many advantages in separating the assessment of these component functions from the task of bringing them to a common scale. Thus non-negative weights w_i are introduced:

$$v(a) = w_1 v_1(a_1) + w_2 v_2(a_2) + \ldots + w_k v_k(a_k)$$
$$= \sum_i w_i v_i(a_i). \tag{4}$$

Comparing (ADD VAL) and (WTADD VAL) shows that apparently all that is being done is to write $w_i v_i(a_i)$ for $v_i(a_i)$, but, in fact, some assumptions are being made about the underlying preferences[3] [DYE79]. Nonetheless, they are assumptions that are usually made and we shall not discuss them here.

Given the structure of the additive value model (WTADD VAL), we can indicate the judgements required of the DM in the assessment of his preferences and the construction of v(a) for each alternative. Roughly, preference judgements need to be elicited in order to construct each of the k component value functions $v_i(.)$ in turn. Then further judgements are required in order to identify appropriate values of the k weights w_i.

For instance, $v_{mem}(.)$ might have the form shown in Figure 7.2 . Its concave (bending downwards) shape indicates that the decision maker values an increase of memory from 8Mb to 9Mb more than he values an increase from 32Mb to 33Mb. This curve could be assessed in a number of ways. Perhaps the most common is to ask the DM for his midpoint in preference between 8Mb and 128Mb: i.e. what is the value xMb such that he values an increase from 8Mb to xMb equally to an increase from xMb to 128Mb? If the scale of $v_{mem}(.)$ is fixed by setting $v_{mem}(8) = 0$ and $v_{mem}(128) = 100$, then it follows that $v_{mem}(x) = 50$. Asking him for his midpoint in preference between 8Mb and xMb locates x/primeMb such that $v_{mem}(x') = 25$. And so on. When sufficient points on $v_{mem}(.)$ have been located, the curve can be sketched in.

The point to note about this assessment is that the DM is required to locate the midpoints by judgement. Although, typically, he is able to do this without too much difficulty, he is usually aware that he is really only able to give a range for the midpoint. Later in the analysis it would be appropriate to return to the assessment and input slightly different midpoints, but ones that are, nevertheless, acceptable to the DM, to see if they would lead to a different conclusion.

---

3   Strictly, we are describing a measurable additive value function, which represents strength of preference between both alternatives a and attribute levels a_i.

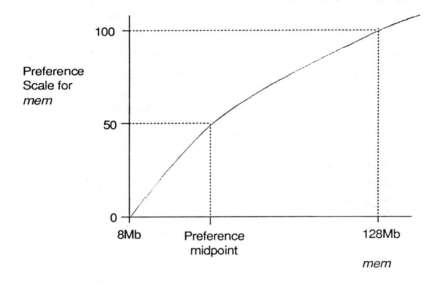

Fig. 7.2 A possible form for $v_{mem}(.)$.

The assessment procedure described here makes sense when (i) there are many alternatives to evaluate and (ii) the levels of the alternatives on the ith attribute can be found easily. When there are only a few alternatives involved in the decision problem, the effort required of the decision maker may be reduced substantially if, instead of constructing $v_i(.)$ for all possible levels of the attribute and then transforming a_i through $v_i(.)$ to give $v_i(a_i)$, the DM is asked to assess $v_i(a_i)$ directly. Moreover, direct assessment of $v_i(a_i)$ is necessary when there is no objective scale for the ith attribute, such as would be the case for the attribute stab in the example. Figure 7.3 illustrates the direct assessment of $v_{stab}(comp\_sys)$.

The DM is asked to rank the alternative computer systems in terms of his preferences for the suppliers' stabilities. Then, scoring his most preferred alternative at, say, 100 and his least preferred at 0, he is asked to score the other alternatives in such a way that his strength of preference between them is reflected in the scores. Figure 7.3 illustrates the result of this in the case that comp_sys_3 is felt to bring as much improvement over comp_sys_6 as comp_sys_1 brings over comp_sys_2: in both cases the difference in point scores is 40.

Again note that the DM is required to locate numerical values by judgement. This usually does not cause him too much difficulty, providing that, as before, he is allowed to return later and investigate the effect of using slightly different values.

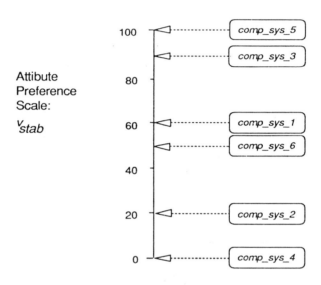

Fig. 7.3 Direct assessment of v_{stab}(comp_sys).

The next step is to assess the weights w_i. It is not simply a case of the DM judging that, say, 'installation costs should carry 30% of the weight'. This would imply that the weights have some sort of absolute values independent of the length of the attribute preference scales. Remember that the greatest and least values of each $v_i(.)$ have been set arbitrarily to 100 and 0, respectively. Weights have two closely entwined roles:

- they represent the relative importance to the decision maker of the different attributes
- they provide an 'exchange rate' between the different attribute preference scales, bringing them onto a common scale.

Swing weighting is an assessment method that takes account of both roles. The DM is asked to compare a pair of hypothetical alternatives which differ only in their scores along two attribute preference scales: on the other $(k-2)$ attributes they share the same scores. Suppose the two attributes on which they differ are disk_acc and perf. The DM is asked to imagine that one alternative scores 100 on disk_acc and 0 on perf and that the other scores 0 on disk_acc and 100 on perf. Which would he prefer? Suppose that he prefers the second. Then a score of 100 on perf is worth more to him than a score of 100 on disk_acc. Hence $w_{perf} > w_{disk\_acc}$. Suppose now he is asked to imagine that the second alternative is modified so that it scores, say, y on perf. Suppose further that the value of y is varied until the DM is indifferent between the two alternatives. Then, if w_{perf} is set to 100, w_{disk_acc} should be set to y/100 because a score of 100 on the disk_acc preference scale is worth a score of y on the perf preference scale.

Figure 7.4 illustrates the essence of swing weighting. If the value of y at which indifference is obtained is, say, 60, then a score of 100 on the disk_acc preference scale maps onto 60 on the perf preference scale.

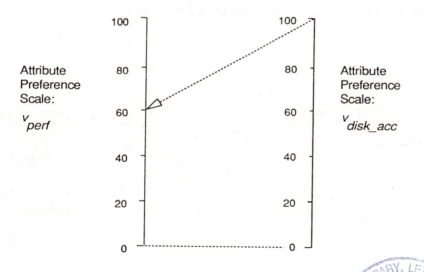

Fig. 7.4 An illustration of swing weights.

By repeating the process on other pairs of hypothetical alternatives a full set of weights can be deduced. In practice it makes sense to begin the process by identifying the attribute with the greatest w_i and then considering the $(k - 1)$ pairs in which this attribute is compared with each of the others in turn.

Yet again note that the DM is required to locate numerical values by judgement. Some investigation of the sensitivity of any conclusions to the effects of varying these will be needed later in the decision analysis.

The next step is to calculate $v(a) = \sum_i w_i v_i(a_i)$ for the alternatives in the decision problem, thus obtaining a preliminary ranking. However, the DM would be wise to take this ranking with a pinch of salt until he has identified how sensitive this ranking is to variations in his judgemental input.

7.3   SENSITIVITY ANALYSIS FOR ADDITIVE VALUE CALCULATIONS

The commonest and most simple form of sensitivity analysis currently used is to examine the effect of varying a single weight. Figure 7.5 illustrates this for the weight w_{run_cost}. The idea is as follows. Suppose that the weights are normalized to sum to 1. Then w_{run_cost} is the fraction of the total weight assigned to the running costs. Suppose that, at present, w_{run_cost} is 35%. This is shown in Figure 7.5 by the dotted vertical line at 35%.

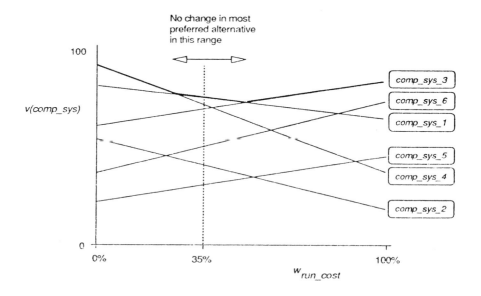

Fig. 7.5   Sensitivity with respect to varying a single weight.

Suppose that w_{run_cost} is varied and all the other weights varied so that (i) the sum of all the weights remains 1 and (ii) the ratios between all pairs of weights not involving w_{run_cost} is maintained. With this understanding one may talk unambiguously of w_{run_cost}, say, increasing to 42% or decreasing to 23%. As w_{run_cost} varies in this manner, so will v(comp_sys) change for each alternative computer system. In fact, v(comp_sys) will vary linearly with w_{run_cost}. Thus a straight line is plotted in Figure 7.5 for each computer system showing the variation of v(comp_sys) with w_{run_cost}. The ordering of the points of intersection of these lines with any vertical corresponds to the ranking given by the additive value function at the particular value of w_{run_cost}. It is, therefore, easy to see the values of w_{run_cost} at which a change in the ranking occurs, namely values corresponding to intersections of two or more v(comp_sys) lines. In particular, values of w_{run_cost} at which the most preferred alternative changes correspond to vertices in the upper envelope of the lines. NB. The upper envelope is shown as a thicker line in Figure 7.5.

We mentioned above that the attribute hierarchy could help in structuring the sensitivity analysis. For instance, the DM could be concerned that he is putting too much weight on non-financial attributes. In the hierarchy shown in Figure 7.1 it is possible to define a weight at the node non-financial simply as the sum of the weights at the bottom nodes below it:

$$w_{non\text{-}financial} = w_{perf} + w_{mem} + w_{disk\_sp} + w_{disk\_acc} + w_{stab}$$
$$+ w_{hard\_rel}. \tag{5}$$

Investigating the sensitivity of the results to $w_{non\text{-}financial}$ will address the DM's concerns.

Standard software packages, such as HIVIEW [HIVIEW], Logical Decision [LD] and VISA [VISA], produce plots similar to Figure 7.5 as a matter of course. VISA also has a particularly nice interactive manner of exploring the same sensitivity effects.

Looking at the expression (WTADD VAL) for the additive value function v(a), it is clear that the effect of varying a single weight w_i is effectively the same as varying the number $v_i(a_i)$. NB. By $v_i(a_i)$ we mean the ith attribute preference scale value for the alternative not a_i, the level this alternative achieves on the ith attribute. When $v_i(a_i)$ has been assessed directly as in Figure 7.3, the DM can investigate the sensitivity of the conclusions to variations in his judgemental input by means of a plot similar to Figure 7.5 with the horizontal axis representing $v_i(a_i)$ instead of w_i. VISA now allows this form of sensitivity analysis. When $v_i(a_i)$ has been assessed indirectly as in Figure 7.2, however, such sensitivity analysis is not necessarily directly related to his judgemental inputs because of the possible non-linear relationship between $v_i(a_i)$ and his judgements of preference midpoints.

One point that should be noted about all these forms of sensitivity analysis is that only one judgemental input is varied at any time. The DM is shown the effect of variations in a particular weight w_i. There is no attempt to investigate the effect of simultaneously and independently varying two or more weights. There certainly is no attempt to investigate simultaneous and independent variation in one or more weights and one or more attribute preference scale values.

7.4   THE ROLE OF SENSITIVITY ANALYSIS

Intuitively, sensitivity calculations allow the DM to explore the effects of variations in his judgemental inputs on the ranking of alternatives produced by the decision analysis. When small variations produce substantial effects, it is clear that the DM should pause and reflect on those judgements and ensure that the numbers used best represent his preferences. When there are no effects even for moderate or large variations, then the DM can be reassured that any uncertainty that he felt in giving those judgements can be ignored. The whole process of sensitivity analysis adds to the DM's understanding of the problem and thus helps him in making his decision.

The results of sensitivity analysis also help the DM in writing a report and explaining his actions to others. He can concentrate on the important issues and not be deflected into lengthy justifications of judgemental inputs that have no significant effect on the final decision.

So far we have considered the case of a single decision maker. In fact, in most cases a group of people are responsible for a decision. This in no way invalidates any of the points in the earlier discussion, but we do need to enlarge the context to the group case. Much decision anlysis is now carried out in decision conferences [FRE89 , Section 4.3], [HAL86], [PHI90]. A decision conference is essentially a two-day event at which a group of people who are responsible for formulating and implementing policy meet to discuss all the major issues and concerns that relate to the problem at hand and to carry out a decision analysis to help them choose a way forward. To help them in their task they are assisted by a facilitator and an analyst who attend to the process and decision modelling, leaving the group free to concentrate on the content of their problem. There are many facets to decision conferencing which need not detain us: our concern is with the role that sensitivity analy sis plays.

During the decision conference the facilitator and analyst will construct a decision model of the choice facing the group. Suppose, for discussion's sake, that they construct an additive value model. The assessment of the judgemental inputs to define the component value functions $v_i(.)$ and the weights w_i will lead to much discussion within the group. Although in many cases consensus will emerge on the values to be used, there will inevitably be disagreement in others. If such disagreements are simply left unresolved, the usefulness of the decision conference will dissipate rapidly because of the discomfort of some of the members with the numerical values used. If an attempt is made to resolve any disagreements through discussion, then the flow of the conference is disrupted and it is possible that deadlock rather than consensus may result. It is far better to suspend discussion and carry on with the analysis using some mean (but not consensus) value. During the sensitivity an alysis phase the results of the model can be examined using a wide range of numerical values for the judgements upon which the group cannot agree. More often than not, it is found that the final ranking of alternatives is unchanged or insignificantly affected by variations across the whole range of numerical values proposed by members. In some cases, of course, significant changes in the ranking do occur and the group must discuss further the numerical values that they will use. Thus sensitivity analysis will focus group discussion on issues that matter and avoid sterile discussion of those that do not.

There are two further aspects to sensitivity analysis that it is appropriate to discuss here. The first is known as the flat maximum principle [WIN86]. Essentially, this is an empirical observation backed up by a 'hand-waving' mathematical argument that, in practice, decision analyses are remarkably robust to judgemental inputs. Moderate variations in the numerical values used seem to have very little effect on the final ranking of alternatives. Undoubtedly, this is in large measure true. However, the inference should not be drawn that sensitivity analyses may be disposed of. Firstly, the decision problem of current concern may be an exception – and exceptions do occur: see Section EXAMPLE below. Secondly, much of the purpose of sensitivity analysis is to bring understanding and reassurance and to focus group discussion. Such benefits will be lost if a sensitivity analysis is not undertaken. Of course, if the tendency to robustness described by the Principle were not to exist, sensitivity analysis would seldom bring understanding, reassure or focus discussion. It would forever be opening cans of worms!

The second point to discuss is why it is better to apply sensitivity analysis to additive value calculations which require precise numerical inputs than to use a decision model which allows the DM to give a range of values for each input. There are models available based on interval orders, fuzzy sets and other techniques which would allow the latter approach. But for me at least, they are unsatisfactory. There are many reasons why I believe this [FRE86]: here I will indicate only the most relevant to our discussion.

Among the assumtions underlying the additive value model is that of transitivity. It is assumed that, if the DM prefers a to b and, in turn, prefers b to c, then he will prefer a to c. There are many arguments in favour of trying to ensure transitivity in ones preferences [FRE86], although it cannot be denied that empirically people do exhibit intransitive preferences. None the less, when intransitivities are brought to their attention, most people — in my experience, all people — revise their judgements in the direction of transitivity.

Suppose that a DM is directly assessing the component value function for an attribute. He might be sure that in terms of this attribute he prefers a to b and b to c. Moreover he might be sure that his preferences are transitive: viz he prefers a to c. He might, however, be uncomfortable in his assessments of particular values for $v_i(a)$, $v_i(b)$ and $v_i(c)$. Suppose that he feels that appropriate numerical values lie in the ranges:

$$70 \quad \leq \quad v_i(a) \quad \leq \quad 85$$
$$60 \quad \leq \quad v_i(b) \quad \leq \quad 75 \tag{6}$$
$$55 \quad \leq \quad v_i(c) \quad \leq \quad 65$$

These ranges allow the possibility:

$$v_i(a) \; 72; \quad v_i(b) = 74; \quad v_i(c) = 58. \tag{7}$$

They also allow:

$$v_i(a) = 75; \quad v_i(b) = 61; \quad v_i(c) = 64. \tag{8}$$

Both these assignments contradict the preference statements made by the DM. Such assignments should, therefore, be excluded from the sensitivity analysis. This can be done easily by constraining all the calculations to satisfy (see Section FRAMEWORK):

$$v_i(a) \quad \geq \quad v_i(b) \quad \geq \quad v_i(c). \tag{9}$$

Decision models which allow ranges of values for each input not only find it difficult to allow constraints of the form (CONSTRAINT), they also can fail to enforce transitivity. Essentially they allow assignment (ASS1) in one part of the analysis, concluding that b is preferred to a; simultaneously in another part of the analysis they allow assignment (ASS2), concluding that c is preferred to b. Yet throughout the analysis they hold that a is preferred to c, because the intervals for $v_i(a)$ and $v_i(c)$ do not overlap. In short, transitivity is lost.

7.5   DECISION ANALYSIS IN THE FACE OF UNCERTAINTY

So far we have focused on decision analyses based on additive value functions. These apply to circumstances in which uncertainty about the outcome of choosing an alternative is not a significant factor. When such uncertainty is an issue then it is appropriate to use subjective probabilities and expected utility analysis [FRE86], [FRE89], [KEE76], [WIN86]. We shall not discuss these methodologies in detail here. We simply wish to make one point. The assessment procedures for subjective probabilities and multi-attribute utility functions make very similar judgemental demands on the DM as do those for additive value functions.

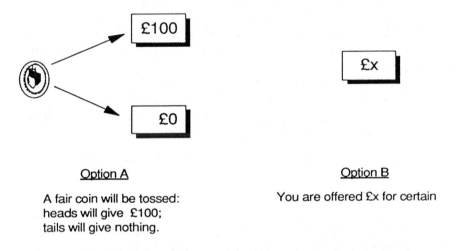

<u>Option A</u>

A fair coin will be tossed: heads will give £100; tails will give nothing.

<u>Option B</u>

You are offered £x for certain

For what value of £x are you indifferent between options A and B?

Fig. 7.6 The assessment of a point on the DM's utility function for monetary gains.

For instance, in assessing utility function for uncertain monetary gains, the DM may be asked a question of the form shown in Figure 7.6 . In practice, of course, the question would not be phrased in such stark terms: Figure 7.6 belongs more to the black and white world of a textbook than the grey landscape of real application. But whatever the wording, the essence is the same: he is asked to give a numerical value which defines a point on his utility curve. It is important, therefore, for all the reasons given in the previous section to conduct a sensitivity analysis on the effect of variations in such judgemental input.

The framework for sensitivity analysis proposed in the next section applies equally to expected utility analysis as to additive value models. In fact, it applies to any paradigm for decision analysis of problems involving a finite number of alternatives.

7.6 A FRAMEWORK FOR SENSITIVITY ANALYSIS

Recently David Rios Insua has developed a framework for sensitivity analysis in multi-criteria decision problems [FRE89B], [RIO90], [RIO91]. This builds on and unifies the work of many others, whose ideas have appeared in the literature over the past 25 years or so: a full bibliography may be found in David Rios Insua's recent monograph [RIO90]. To explain the framework, we shall need a little mathematical notation.

A survey of the methods proposed in the literature for sensitivity investigations of decision analytic calculations leads to two general conclusions.

- The majority of proposals are ad hoc in that they apply to particular decision models and do not generalise transparently to others.
- One or at most two judgemental inputs are varied at a time, yet there may be a hundred or more such inputs involved in a decision analysis.

Let us assume that the DM has to choose from a finite set of alternatives:

$$A = \{a, b, c, \dots\}.$$

We assume that the decision analytic model used ranks the alternatives via an evaluation function $\psi(a,\omega)$. By this we mean that the model suggests that alternative a should be preferred to alternative b if:

$$\psi(a, \omega) \geq \psi(b, \omega),$$

where $\omega = (\omega_1, \omega_2, \dots, \omega_p)$ is the vector of judgemental inputs made by the DM during the assessment process. For instance, in the assessment of an additive value function (WTADD VAL) ω would comprise preference midpoints used to determine the k component value functions $v_i(.)$, any directly assessed component values $v_i(a_i)$, and the k weights w_i. If an expected utility model were being used, ω would comprise judgemental numerical values which determine the subjective probabilities as well as the multi-attribute utility model. Typically, p, the number of judgemental inputs, will be between twenty and two hundred or so.

As we noted in the discussion of transitivity in Section 7.4, the DM will usually provide more information than simple numerical values for each element of ω. There will almost certainly be ranges for each input − not precise ranges, for it is as difficult judgementally to give a precise range for a numerical value as to give the value itself precisely. Rather these ranges will derive from statements made by the DM such as:

'Set $v_{stab}(comp\_sys\_1)$ at 60. I am sure that it is above 50 but not too much above. I wouldn't set it as high as 70.'

Such a statement would give inequality constraints:

$$50 < v_{stab}(comp\_sys\_1) < 70,$$

but there would be no claims that 50 and 70 were tight bounds. There may also be constraints such as (CONSTRAINT) arising from transitivity; the DM will often identify an ordering of the weights on the attribute scales; and so on.

As a result of the assessment process the analyst will have determined from the DM an initial numerical value for each of the judgemental inputs and some constraints limiting other values that the DM would also find acceptable. Let ω^o be the initial judgemental values given by the DM and let S denote the constraint set so determined. Thus the DM would wish to explore judgemental inputs /omega lying in S.

Three concepts built around the use of the set S will concern us here. Firstly, it may be that some alternatives are better than others whatever values of the judgemental inputs are used, subject to the values remaining in S. In such circumstances we shall say that a dominates b. Put mathematically, a dominates b if:

$$\psi(a,\omega) \geq \psi(b,\omega), \quad \forall \omega \in S. \tag{10}$$

The concept of dominance follows simply from the application of standard Pareto ordering ideas to the present context, and we are far from the first to suggest its use here: see, e.g., [HAZ86]. What distinguishes the approach that follows from previous work is that we use ω and S to describe all the judgemental inputs of the DM. Previous approaches have focused on subsets of the judgemental inputs: e.g. they have considered only the weights and taken all other judgementally set quantities as fixed. This remark is particularly pertinent to suggestions that have been made for sensitivity investigations of expected utility models: either the subjective probabilities have been taken as fixed and the utilities varied or *vice versa.*

The second concept identifies those alternatives that could be optimal for some acceptable values of the judgemental inputs. We shall say that such alternatives are potentially optimal (p.o.). In mathematical terms: a is p.o. if for some $\omega \in S$,

$$\psi(a,\omega) \geq \psi(b,\omega), \quad \forall b \in A. \tag{11}$$

It seems sensible to confine the DM's attention to nondominated, p.o. alternatives.

The third concept is that of adjacent potential optimality (a.p.o.). The initial judgemental inputs ω^0 are not arbitrary. They represent values with which the DM is, in some sense, most comfortable. As the decision analysis progresses and sensitivity is investigated, the DM may reflect upon these values and change them as his understanding is enhanced. We shall slightly change the definition of ω^0 to accommodate this. ω^0 will be the values of the judgemental inputs that the DM currently feels the most appropriate to use in the analysis. A question that will constantly concern the DM is: how much must his judgements change from ω^0 before a different alternative becomes optimal? Suppose that a^0 is the alternative that is currently ranked first:

$$\psi(a^0,\omega^0) \geq \psi\,(b,\omega^0), \quad \forall\, b \in A. \tag{11}$$

We shall call b an a.p.o. alternative to a if it is possible to change ω smoothly away from ω^0 in such a manner that a^0 and b interchange as the optimal alternative. Note that this does not necessarily mean that b is ranked second at $\omega = \omega^0$. For instance, that in Figure 7.5 *comp_sys_3* is a.p.o. to *comp_sys_1* but ranked third at when w_{run_cost} is 35%. The mathematical formulation requires that we define some subsets of S. Let S^0 be the subset of S for which a^0 is optimal and, generally, let S^b be the subset of S for which b is optimal. Then b is a.p.o. to a^0 if $S^0 \cap S^b \neq \varnothing$.

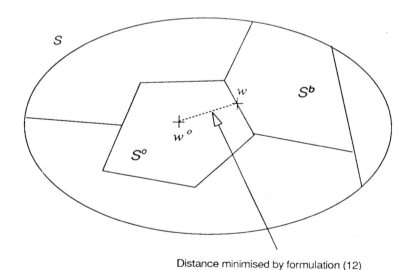

Distance minimised by formulation (12)

Fig. 7.7 Adjacent potential optimality in terms of subsets of S.

Figure 7.7 illustrates the idea. Essentially b is a.p.o. to a^o if S^o and S^b share a common boundary.

Adjacent potential optimality informs the DM which alternatives are immediate contenders with a^o for optimality, but it does not tell him how close a contender each is. Suppose that b is a.p.o. to a^o. Let $\omega \in S^b$: i.e. let ω be one possible assignment of judgemental inputs for which b is optimal. Then the smaller $|\omega - \omega^o|$, the closer a contender to a^o is b. Hence for each a.p.o. alternative b to a^o we solve the following minimisation problem: see Figure 7.7.

$$\text{minimise} \ | \ \omega - \omega^o \ | \\ \omega \in S^b \tag{12}$$

The minimum value of $| \ \omega - \omega^o \ |$, in a sense, answers the question of how 'close' a contender b is. Of course, this begs a further question: what metric, i.e. definition of distance, should we use to measure $| \ \omega - \omega^o \ |$? At present, we have no clear answer to this. Our methods allow the use of a number of metrics and, in practice, we examine the results for several.

Thus the scheme that we propose for sensitivity analysis involves the following steps.

1. Identify the nondominated alternatives.

2. Find which of these are potentially optimal.

3. Find the adjacent potentially optimal alternatives to a^o and in each case the least change in ω needed for optimality to switch.

Before giving an example, perhaps one last point should be made. In practice, assessment of judgemental inputs and sensitivity analyses of the results will iterate: see Figure 7.8. Our view of decision analysis is fully in accord with Phillips' notion of requisite decision modelling [PHI84].

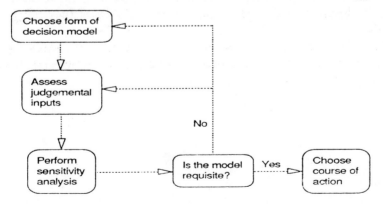

Fig. 7.8 The iterative interplay between assessment and sensitivity analysis.

7.7   AN EXAMPLE

In this Section we examine the sensitivity of an additive value model used to evaluate flood plain management options [GOI82]. For simplicity, we only consider variations in the weights. The generality of our approach is not, therefore, illustrated. Indeed, we do no more than has been proposed by, inter alia, Hazen [HAZ86]. An analysis which varies both the weights and the attribute preference scale values may be found in [RIO90 , Sections 7.2 and 7.5]

The additive value model was used to help the City of Dallas choose between eight alternative flood plain management plans:

1. **No Action** *(No_act)* Leave the flood plain management as it is.
2. **Purchase the Flood Plain** *(Buy)* Buy all areas liable to be flooded and relocate residents.
3. **A Park Greenway: North** *(Park_N)* Develop parkland for recreational purposes in the north of the Flood Plain.
4. **A Park Greenway: South** *(Park_S)* As Park_N, but in the south of the flood plain.
5. **A Basic Greenway** *(Green)* Widen current channel.
6. **A Concrete Channel** *(Con_Ch)* Build a concrete channel along the present channel.
7. **A Bypass Channel** *(Bypass)* Build a channel to bypass the area.
8. **Purchase and Redevelop the Flood Plain** *(Redev)* Purchase the flood plain and undertake major redevelopment.

Goicoechea et al. [GOI82] describe the alternatives in greater detail, but their precise definition need not concern us. What matters is that we appreciate that the alternatives differ greatly. Each of them represents a distinctly different course of action and in many cases they are mutually exclusive.

The alternatives were scored against the ten attributes shown in Figure 7.9. Table 1 gives the scores used, as well as the weights applied to these attribute scores.

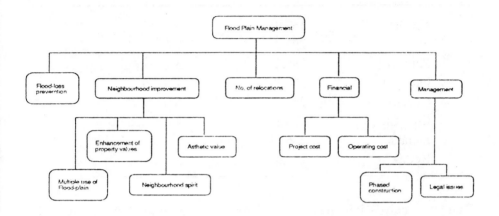

Fig. 7.9 The attributes used in the Dallas Flood Plain Example.

Table 7.1 Attribute preference scores and weights.

| | Prevention | | Prop_Val | Asthetic | | Proj_cost | | Phasing | | |
		Mult-Use		Nghd-Sprt	Reloc'ns		Opns_cost			Legal
No_act	1	3	1	1	1	1.0	8.0	6.0	8	2
Buy	6	7	5	4	2	8.0	2.8	8.0	7	2
Park_N	5	5	7	7	7	5.9	4.0	1.0	4	7
Park_S	6	6	8	8	8	4.3	3.3	1.0	4	6
Green	4	4	4	5	5	6.6	4.7	1.0	3	5
Con_Ch	8	2	3	2	4	7.4	5.6	5.3	2	4
Bypass	4	3	3	3	4	7.7	2.7	8.0	1	8
Redev	7	8	6	6	6	2.7	1.0	1.0	6	1
Weights	10	7	3	5	6	8	9	4	2	1

Using the additive value formula to rank the alternatives gives the results shown in Table 7.2.

Table 7.2 Attribute preference scores and weights.

	Total Score	Rank
No_act	167.0	8
Buy	293.2	2
Park_N	285.2	3
Park_S	296.1	1
Green	245.1	6
Con_Ch	275.8	4
Bypass	236 .9	7
Redev	257.6	5

Thus the analysis initially suggests Park_S as the optimal choice. It is also clear that Buy is close to Park_S in terms of total score: but this does not necessarily mean that the optimality of Park_S is sensitive to changes in the judgemental inputs. It might be that changes that increase the total score of Buy also increase the total score of Park_S.

From the information given in [GOI82] the only constraints on the weights were that they should be non-negative. To illustrate the methods we assume the following upper and lower bounds on the weights:

$$5 \leq \text{WPrevention} \leq 20,$$
$$4 \leq \text{WMult-Use} \leq 10,$$
$$0 \leq \text{WProp\_Val} \leq 15,$$
$$5 \leq \text{WAsthetic} \leq 10,$$
$$0 \leq \text{WNghd\_Sprt} \leq 10,$$
$$5 \leq \text{WReloc'ns} \leq 10,$$
$$5 \leq \text{WProj\_Cost} \leq 15,$$
$$3 \leq \text{WOpns\_Cost} \leq 5,$$
$$0 \leq \text{WPhasing} \leq 3,$$
$$0 \leq \text{WLegal} \leq 5.$$

We also assume the following constraints:

$0 \leq$ WPrevention $+$ WMult-Use $+$ WProp_Val $-$ WAsthetic $-$ WNghd_Sprt

$0 \leq$ WPrevention $-$ WMult-Use $+$ WProp_Val $+$ WAsthetic $+$ WOpns_Cost WPhasing $-$ WLegal

$0 \leq$ WReloc'ns $+$ WProj_Cost $+$ WOpns_Cost $-$ WPhasing $-$ WLegal

Finally, to avoid unboundedness we constrain the weights to sum to 55. Given these constraints, the set of nondominated alternatives is:

{Buy, Park_N, Park_S, Con_Ch, Bypass, Redev},

and the set of nondominated p.o. alternatives is:

{Buy, Park_N, Park_S, Con_Ch, Redev}.

The set of alternatives which are a.p.o. to Park_S is:

{Buy, Park_N, Con_Ch, Redev}.

Under a range of metrics Buy is the nearest a.p.o. alternative to Park_S: for numerical details see [RIO90 , pp 136-141]. Very small changes in the weights lead to Buy becoming optimal. For instance, Table 7.3 compares the initial weights with a set of weights making Buy and Park_S jointly optimal and Figure FIG9A shows a plot of the changes needed. Clearly the decision is very sensitive to the choice of weights.

Table 7.3 Weights which make Park_S and Buy jointly optimal.

	Prevention	Prop_Val	Asthetic		Proj_cost		Phasing		
		Mult-Use	Nghd-Sprt		Reloc'ns		Opns_cost		Legal
Park_S	10.0	7.0	3.0	5.0	6.0	8.0	9.0	4.0	2.0	1.0
Both	10.0	7.1	2.9	5.0	5.9	8.1	8.9	4.1	2.1	0.9

There is a much more detailed sensitivity analysis of this example in [RIO90, Sections 7.2 and 7.5]. There the closeness of all a.p.o. alternatives to Park_S is examined. Moreover, it is shown that much the same conclusions can be drawn whatever metric is used to define 'closeness'. Other ways of displaying the changes in the judgemental inputs needed to cause optimality to switch are suggested, and the possibility of devising a sensitivity index discussed. However, without such further analysis it should be clear that the decision to adopt the Park_S alternative is far from robust to small changes in judgemental inputs. Such a conclusion would inform a decision analysis and concentrate the DMs' minds on critical issues.

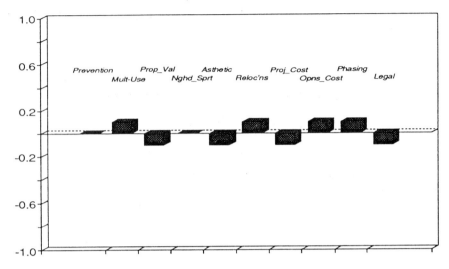

Fig. 7.10 A histogram showing the changes needed to make Buy optimal

7.8   A VIEW OF THE FUTURE?

The methods that we are proposing are far from easy computationally. Essentially they require the solution of a large number of mathematical programmes (constrained optimisation problems). For instance, simply identifying the non-dominated alternatives in the example of the previous section required the solution of seventeen linear programmes. Moreover, although many of the mathematical programmes may be linear, far from all are. Some are bilinear, and non-convex, non-linear programmes can arise. Solving these problems on a PC would be so time consuming that interactive decision analysis would be infeasible. David Rios Insua has produced a demonstrator sensitivity analysis package running on an Amdahl 5860 mainframe [RIO90]. However, such a computational resource is unlikely to be available to decision analysts in a decision conference.

A way forward is to use parallel processing based upon transputers on a card mounted in a PC host. See Figure 7.10. Such hardware is rapidly falling in price, providing the raw computing power needed away from mainframe environments. More importantly, parallel processing approaches are ideally suited to the problem of solving of many similar mathematical programmes. By this we do not mean the parallelisation of the solution algorithms for the mathematical programmes. Rather we have a more macro-approach in mind. The solution of individual mathematical programmes would be farmed out to individual transputers. SERC has awarded a research grant to a group of us working at Leeds to investigate such an approach.

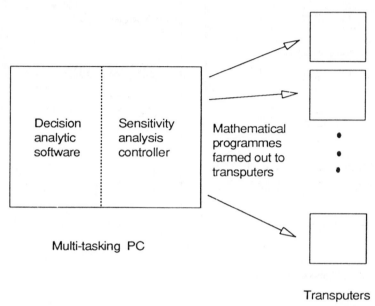

Fig. 7.11 A transputer system for implementing the framework.

Our intention is to run decision analytic software such as HIVIEW, Logical Decision or VISA in the foreground on the PC. As sensitivity analyses become necessary, these would be organised and farmed out to the transputers as background processes. The results of these analyses would be presented to the decision analyst through a window which would pop-up as they became available. Indeed, we would expect all the tools of decision analysis to be made available through a windowing environment: see Figure 7.12.

It would be foolish to pretend that all this will be available in a month or two. There are difficulties to be addressed, choices to be made and much programming to be done. But we do believe that within two or three years a parallel processing implementation of the sensitivity analysis framework presented here will be able to tackle realistically sized problems in (near) real time.

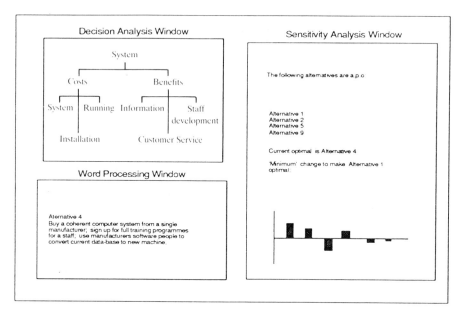

Fig. 7.12   The screen.

7.9   ACKNOWLEDGEMENTS

I am grateful to Les Proll, David Rios Insua, Abdellah Salhi and Doug White for many helpful discussions. David Rios Insua performed the computations for the example of Section 7.7.

REFERENCES

Barclay, S., HIVIEW Decision Analysis Unit, London School of Economics and Political Science, Houghton Street, London.

Belton, V. and Vickers, S. VISA.

Dyer, J. S. and Sarin, R. K. (1979) Measurable multi-attribute value functions, *Operations Research,* 22, 810-822.

French, S. (1986) Decision Theory: An Introduction to the Mathematics of Rationality, Ellis Horwood, Chichester.

French, S. (1989) *Readings in Decision Analysis*, Chapman and Hall, London.

French, S. and Rios Insua, D. (1989) Partial information and sensitivity analysis in multi-objective decision-making, in G. Lockett and G.Islei (eds), *Improving Decision Making in Organisations.*

Goicoechea, A., Hansen, D.R. and Duckstein, L. *Multi-Objective Decision Analysis with Engineering and Business Applications,* John Wiley, New York.

Hall, P. (1986) Managing change and gaining corporate commitment, *ICL Technical Journal,* 7, 213-227.

Hazen, G. B. (1986) Partial information, dominance and potential optimality in multi-attribute utility theory, *Operations Research,* 34, 296-310.

Keeney, R. L. and Raiffa, H. (1976) *Decisions with Multiple Objectives: Preferences and Value Tradeoffs,* John Wiley, New York.

Phillips, L. D. (1984) A theory of requisite decision models, *Acta Psychologica,* 56, 29-48.

Phillips, L.D. (1990) Decision analysis for group decision support, in C. Eden and J. Radford (eds), *Tackling Strategic Problems: The Role of Group Decision Support,* Sage, London.

Rios Insua, D. (1990) Sensitivity Analysis in *Multi-Objective Decision Making Lecture Notes in Mathematics and Economic Systems,* Springer Verlag.

Rios Insua, D. and French, S. (1991) A framework for sensitivity analysis in discrete multi-objective decision-making, *European Journal of Operational Research* (in press).

Smith, G.R. *Logical Decision,* Logical Decisions, 164 E. Scenic Ave., Point Richmond, CA 94801, USA.

von Winterfeldt, D. and Edwards, W. (1986) *Decision Analysis and Behavioural Research,* Cambridge University Press, Cambridge.

8 Supporting multi-criteria decision making

New perspectives and new systems

A. A. Angehrn
European Institute of Business Administration

More and more researchers in Information and Decision Support Systems recognize that the field of computer-based decision making is changing. The new challenge can be characterized by a 'humanization' of decision support, i.e. by the attempt to 'humanize' the way a DSS interacts with its users and the form in which it delivers to them decision-supporting knowledge in different forms (data, rules, models and other techniques).

The new perspectives, together with design guidelines and a concrete example of such a 'humanized' DSS, are discussed in this paper with a special emphasis on the prototypic field of supporting multiple criteria decision making.

Keywords: Decision making, DSS, Human-Computer Interaction, MCDM (multi-criteria decision making).

8.1 SUPPORTING MULTI-CRITERIA DECISIONS

Multi-criteria decisions pose dilemmas or even crises of judgements: ethical choices, tradeoffs between cost and service, conflicts of preferences and 'political' problems are obvious examples. The multicriteria problem is at the core of Decision Support (Keen 1987).

As testified by the above quotation, everyday human decision making typically involves the consideration of more than one single criterion. Accordingly, multi-criteria decision making (MCDM) has been widely studied in Management Science/Operations Research (see, e.g., Zeleny 1982; Edwards and Newman 1982; Saaty 1986; Roy 1971 or Keeney and Raiffa 1976 as examples of the very large MCDM literature) and the resulting theories and methods have been applied in several fields, such as marketing, group decision support and computer-assisted negotiation (Bui and Jarke 1985; Jarke et al. 1987).

At the same time these studies have stimulated the development of computer-based systems aiming at the interactive support of multi-criteria decision making. These systems are generally classified as Decision Support Systems (DSS; cf. Keen and Scott Morton 1978 as a classical work on DSS, or the more recent Sprague and Watson 1989 and Turban 1988 and specifically called Multi-criteria Decision Support Systems (MCDSS; cf. Jelassi et al. 1985 or a survey in Eom 1989).

One of the main motivations for the work reported in this paper has been the diffuse dissatisfaction with the existing approaches to understand, model and support MCDM:

Why are the developed MCDM theories well known, used and generally accepted almost without criticism only in the academic field? Why — if multi-criteria decision situations are so common — does the number of managers/decision makers effectively using MCDSS remain practically insignificant? *Summa summarum*: What is wrong with these scientific approaches to MCDM and with the resulting MCDSS?

A polemical, but very clear answer to these questions, has been proposed by Zeleny (1989) in the following terms:

Mostly, we have imposed a mathematical artefact, both simple and simpleminded in its design, on the rich, natural, self-organizing and knowledge-producing processes of individual and social decision making, without even attempting for its deeper understanding.

The very triviality of this 'paradigm' makes it self-evident and thus beyond criticism. Define a set (given, closed and/or convex) of fixed, well-defined alternatives, assign a number to each of its components according to a more or less complex (utility, preference) function or rule, then search (algorithmically) and identify the alternative(s) receiving the largest number.

Label this mechanism and search routine Decision Making and its perpetrator as the Decision Maker (DM). Base most of your economic, financial and psychological theories on this remarkable insight into the 'nature of things'.

In full agreement with the above statement, we believe that the major pitfall of traditional approaches to MCDM and MCDSS lies in the assumption that human decision-making processes can be reduced to mere 'problem-solving' routines, whereas 'problems' are perceived as object realities which can be modelled by the skilled analyst and 'solved' by applying developing formal techniques reproducing/simulating what has been idealized as rational behaviour.

In addition, we noted that the criticism applied to traditional MCDM approaches — although generating interesting 'philosophical' discussions — has been almost never accompanied by new, constructive perspectives in the form of concrete alternatives for approaching and supporting multi-criteria decision making.

By briefly discussing the conceptual basis (*Weltanschauung*) and the design principles underlying the development of a new system called 'Triple C', this paper aims at demonstrating that such a concrete alternative exists and that it effectively leads to a different type of DSS.

Furthermore it should be noted that the application of the principles discussed in the following is not limited to the MCDM domain but can be successfully employed in other contexts for supporting human decision making through interactive computer- based systems, as reported in Angehrn (1989) and Angehrn and Luthi (1990).

The remainder of the paper is structured into three paragraphs presenting our approach through a decision of the three concepts contained in the acronym DSS, i.e.:

● The adoption of an alternative perspective to 'Decision' making (part 2);
● the related, alternative way of delivering 'Support' (part 3);
● the different characteristics of the resulting 'Systems' (part 4).

In part 5, the guidelines described in this paper will be illustrated by a concrete example: the visual interactive MCDSS called 'Triple C'.

8.2 LEARNING VS. SOLVING: TOWARDS DIFFERENT DECISION-MAKING MODELS

As discussed in the previous paragraph, one of the main problems with the traditional approach to support human decision making is the neglect of the 'human', or cognitive aspects. Aiming at being as 'scientific ' as possible (cf. concepts such as objectivity, rationality and optimality), the traditional perspective tends to reduce the influence of human components such as subjectivity and creativity, and it approaches decision-making processes as if they were identical to technical problem-solving processes.

Usually, a first phase of problem identification (often performed by an external expert/analyst) is followed by a deduction step in which the decision situation is reduced to a formal problem and then solved. This mainly sequential process is illustrated in Figure 8.1 together with the classical, widely referenced 'Intelligence-Design-Choice' model proposed by Simon (1960).

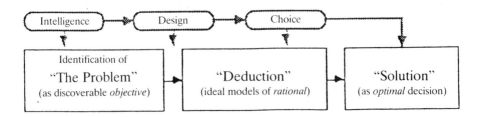

Fig. 8.1 The traditional 'solving' perspective.

A similar approach is also generally adopted in the MCDM field: first, decision makers are asked to express their 'preference structure' in different forms, e.g. by weighting different criteria, by specifying a holistic ranking of a subset of alternatives or by answering questions about their preferences. This information serves then as an input to the model(s) which have been developed and *a priori* embedded into the MCDSS and whose output will generally deliver an 'optimal' ranking of the available alternatives, i.e. the 'best' decision to take.

The main dimensions in which the perspective adopted in our work differs from the one previously described are:

1. Decision situations are not viewed as problems (which can be objectively formulated and solved) but as processes (which start from a subjective perception of an unsatisfactory real-world condition).

2. Decision making is not interpreted in terms of a procedure for deducing the best solution, but as a continually evolving, individual learning process (cf. the work of Checkland (1985) as well as the work of Courbon (1984) relating decision making to Piaget's theories of learning).

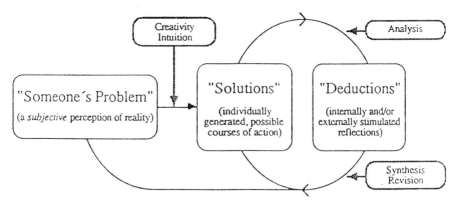

Fig. 8.2 The alternative 'learning' perspective.

Accordingly, the model depicted in Figure 8.2 offers an alternative to the traditional one (Figure 8.1). In this model the key elements (as opposed to the three classical phases 'intelligence', 'design' and 'choice' are:

a. Creativity and intuition

i.e. the human capabilities of generating 'solutions' starting from a (more or less) vague perception that 'something should be done' or 'something should happen', i.e. the formulation of possible courses of action even in the absence of a well structured, clearly and completely formulated problem statement.

b. A learning cycle driven by

analytical steps, in which human reflection or alternatively the need of communicating/justifying the own choices stimulates decision makers in continuously questioning the own 'solutions', reinforcing the existing ones or even leading to a revision of previous perceptions and to a new or more precise 'problem' formulation.

8.3 AN ALTERNATIVE APPROACH TO DELIVERING 'SUPPORT'

It is obvious that the two different perspectives described in part 2 led to different interpretations of how a decision-making process should be supported (by a computer-based instrument as well as in more general terms).

According to the first, traditional, perspective supporting a decision process mainly consists in delivering to a decision maker a set of good problem-solving techniques (efficient mathematical methods, fast information retrieval techniques, inference mechanisms etc.). This tendency can be observed in the majority of today's DSS (and MCDSS). In spite of the often repeated but seldom applied original 'dreams' – user first-technology second, support rather than replace, deal with unstructured tasks, etc. – these systems still remain strongly technology-driven, as attested by the use of terms such as 'data-oriented' and 'model-oriented' (Alter 1977) for classifying different DSS types.

The 'learning' perspective proposed in part 2 asks for a different kind of support which will be discussed here in the specific MCDM context. In supporting incremental processes as the one displayed in Figure 8.2, 'solving' techniques only play a secondary role. The primary support component consists in facilitating decision makers to progressively gain insights into the situation they are faced with by providing different tools enabling them:

1. To understand better the decision situation at hand by expressing and analysing their own preference structures, testing different alternatives and comparing them interactively.

2. To question and verify their individual judgement by performing different types of sensitivity analysis.

3. To justify their subjective choices and communicate them easily — a crucial factor in group decisions.

As a result, an MCDSS should primarily have the characteristics of a 'flexible environment in which individual learning about a decision situation can take place'.

This implies that — independently from specific, predefined solving of information processing techniques — these systems should offer to their users:

a. The possibility (and tools) for describing/modelling their own views of the decision situation at hand (cf. Geoffrion (1989), Jones (1989), as well as the concept of 'modelling primitives' in Angehrn (1989)).

b. The flexibility to access different information processing techniques according to their own cognitive style in order to refine their views in an incremental process and to develop their own strategies in exploring and generating different decision alternatives (cf. the concept of 'Modelling by example' in Angehrn (1989)).

In summary, the two main roles (or support dimensions) an (MC)DSS should play in order to support an evolutive decision-making process are (Figure 8.3):

1. A facilitator role

i.e. tools enabling decision makers to easily express/represent their views and ideas interactively using the available information.

2. A stimulator role

i.e. tools stimulating an incremental reviewing/learning process and hence enabling decision-makers to easily process the information at hand.

8.4   GUIDELINES FOR 'SYSTEM' DESIGN

The two different perspectives described in part 2 not only influence the kind of 'support' to be given to a decision maker, but also the methodology followed in designing and developing computer-based systems for this purpose.

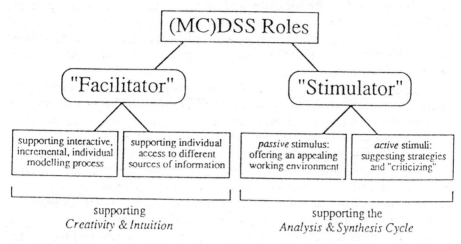

Fig. 8.3 DSS support dimensions.

The kind of support offered in the first case (traditional 'solving' perspective) generally leads to the design of methods — or data-centred systems. The essence of such systems consists in a specific solving technique (e.g. database access methods).

As discussed in Angehrn (1989) these systems generally result from a 'techno-centred' design focusing on determining the functionality (models, methods and data) presumably needed by the decision maker and then embedding it into the system with the eventual addition of a so-called 'user-friendly' interface (cf. the left side of Figure 8.4).

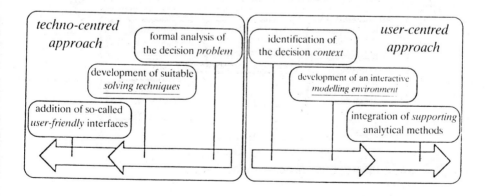

Fig. 8.4 Techno-centred vs. user-centred DSS design.

Adopting the second perspective requires on theother hand the design of a computer-based environment whose main characteristic is not to deliver functionality but to be flexible and usable enough for accompanying (facilitating and stimulating, as described before) a user-driven learning process. Accordingly, the 'user-centred' design depicted on the right-hand side of Figure 8.4 summarizes an alternative to the classical, 'techno-centred' design style.

For instance, the first step in MCDM design consists in identifying the major information processing which could be performed by decision makers in exploring a multi-criteria situation. An overview of these main activities (potential scope of action) is represented in Figure 8.5.

The second step then consists of designing an environment and supporting a decision maker to easily and flexibly perform the different activities identified in the previous step. Such environments should be designed taking into account the cognitive aspects of human information processing as well as existing/accepted ways of performing the task, trying to recreate on the screen a context matching as much as possible the mental models of the decision maker (cf. Winograd and Flores (1986) and Norman and Draper (1986) and note the difference between 'user-centred' system design and the widely used, but superficial concept of 'user-friendliness').

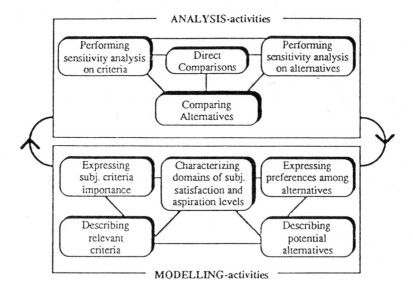

Fig. 8.5 Main information-processing activities.

8.5   FROM THEORY TO PRACTICE: THE 'TRIPLE C' SYSTEM

8.5.1 Building effective visual interactive systems

As recognized even in the DSS research field (cf. Turban and Carlson (1989); Angehrn and Luthi (1990) and Bell et al. (1984), Visual Interaction is a powerful concept for designing environments with the above-mentioned characteristics in which an effective human-computer communication /cooperation plays a crucial role. As a matter of fact, visual interactive systems allow a flexible, natural, 'user-driven' processing of information:

a.   Visual Interaction adds a concrete dimension to information.

   Associating symbolic (e.g. iconic), visual representations to data and data-processing mechanisms diminish the degree of abstraction in exploring and processing different sources of information and facilitates their dynamic organization according to the decision maker's cognitive style.

b. Visual Interaction relies on a familiar mental model.

   Human-computer interaction takes place following the well-known rules of physical interaction with real-world objects, giving to the decision maker a feeling of directness – 'direct manipulation', 'wysiwyg' (Schneiderman 1987) – and transparency through immediate visual feedbacks (Norman and Draper 1986).

c.   Visual Interaction supports environments support a parallel, dynamic style of information processing enhancing associative thinking, experimentation and creativity.

Furthermore, the development of visual interactive systems can be naturally embedded in the 'user-centred' design illustrated on the right-hand side of Figure 8.4. Visual interactive systems are not simply traditional, 'techno-centred' systems masked with a colourful graphic-based, user-friendly interface! On the contrary, they result from a 'user-centred' design whose main concern is to identify first a suitable level of human-computer interaction based on visualization and direct manipulation of the different sources of information which are relevant for the decision maker.

   The integration of different degrees of system functionality – database access, mathematical models and methods as well as Artificial Intelligence techniques as described in Angehrn (1989) – takes place only in the final, third step, as summarized in Figure 8.6.

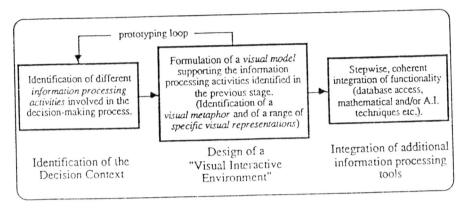

Fig. 8.6 Visual interactive system design.

A concrete demonstration of a system resulting from adopting such a visual interactive approach is presented in the next section through the description of the main characteristics of the 'Triple C' system.

8.5.2 'Triple C': the main characteristics

'Triple C' (Angehrn 1990) is a visual interactive system supporting multi-criteria decision-making processes. Starting from the objectives described in part 2 (individual learning vs. generic problem solving) the kind of support delivered by 'Triple C' is oriented to facilitate incremental problem structuring, individual exploration of the space of alternatives and easy communication of the results of a decision-making process.

Accordingly, the first main characteristic of 'Triple C' consists in not restricting the decision makers with predefined, fixed structures during the phases of problem specification, of generation of possible solutions, and of their incremental analysis. The stimulus of the system consists in supplying to the decision makers a flexible environment equipped with attractive, intuitively clear tools allowing them to perform easily the different modelling and analysis activities described in part 4 (Figure 8.5) according to their own cognitive style. In this way the decision makers are encouraged in describing their own problem views and in developing individual strategies for exploring the decision situation at hand and gaining insights into it.

This user-driven process is substantially facilitated by the second main characteristics of 'Triple C': immediate visual feedbacks enable the users to process different pieces of information simultaneously and to see immediately the propagation and the consequences of changes. This is a first result of the application of such a visual interactive approach, as outlined in part 5.1.

Information processing becomes analogous to the exploration of a physical system in which the different system components can be made visible and in which every manipulation of change is followed by a visible, easily understandable, immediate feedback. (Move the pedal of the bicycle and you will immediately see that something will happen the chain, the back wheel and eventually the whole bike!) This kind of systems transparency is a direct effect of using a suitable form of visual interaction (Norman and Draper 1986) and will be discussed later in the more important context of integrating mathematical techniques into Decision Support Systems.

The consequent use of a visual language (Chang 1986) is a further element that contributes to facilitating systems control and to the enhancement of the 'learning' process illustrated in Figure 8.2. In 'Triple C', the visual-based interaction language is embedded in a generic 'desktop' metaphor (Smith et al. 1982) which supports the computer user in manipulating and organizing different information sources on the screen as if they were physical objects lying on his or her desk (sheets of paper, folders, graphics, etc.). Following the design approach of Figure 8.6, different task-specific (MCDM-specific) visual representations have been designed in order to enable users to represent and analyse a decision without being obliged to memorize an abstract command language and avoiding the danger of getting lost in a complex 'menu-first'.

Figure 8.7 illustrates two examples of such visual aids. The concrete example refers to the application of 'Triple C' to a recruitment problem where the decision maker has to choose between different candidates for a specific job considering different criteria, such as experience, salary expectations, a test score, the decision maker's impression after an interview, etc. The two visual tools displayed in Figure 8.7 permit the users to:

a. Define and monitor the different criteria involved in the decision, as well as assign weights to the single criteria.

   In 'Triple C' each criterion is represented by a sector as displayed on the left-hand side of Figure 8.7. The size (radius) of each sector visually indicates the importance of a criterion in respect to the others. Decision makers can interactively modify the size of the single sectors adapting the criteria's importance to their own subjective view.

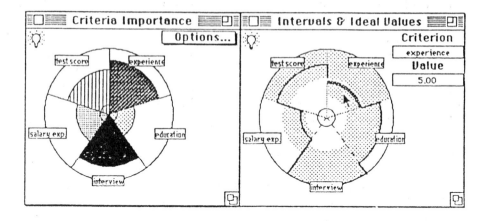

Fig. 8.7 Visual tools allowing to express individual preferences.

b. Express their preferences by specifying intervals of 'feasible' values.

For instance, through the visual representation displayed on the right hand side of Figure 8.7, the decision maker can easily express that a 'feasible' candidate for the job should have experience of at least two years, a salary expectation of between $60,000 and $80,000, and several other conditions associated with each single criterion.

c. Specify 'ideal' values (aspiration levels) for each single criterion considered during the decision-making process.

For instance, using again the visual representation displayed on the right-hand side of Figure 8.7, the decision maker can specify that an 'ideal' candidate for the job should have five years of experience, a salary expectation of $65,000, etc.

Visual representations such as the ones displayed in Figure 8.7 contribute to supplying an additional, visual dimension to information (Angehrn 1990) The numerous 'Triple C' tools make information easier to handle, to interpret (e.g. through a visual comparison of alternatives) and to communicate in a group (cf. the concept of 'wysiwis − What You See Is What I See − as an approach for designing group interfaces (Stefik et al. 1987)).

A last characteristic of 'Triple C' which is extremely relevant in the context of the issues discussed in this paper is the smooth integration of mathematical techniques into the decision-making process.

As discussed in Angehrn (1989), mathematical methods and other complex information-processing techniques also play an important role in the 'learning' perspective described in part 2. In this context, their integration into a DSS is not oriented to substitute and replace human judgement, but − according to Figure 8.3 − to actively stimulate decision makers to gain more insight into the space of alternatives and to explore different possibilities for improving the 'quality' of their solutions (i.e. to identify solutions they feel more comfortable with and that they can more easily justify and explain).

The mathematical techniques embedded in 'Triple C' aim at supporting the users in performing visual-based sensitivity analysis and hence giving a better understanding of their own preference structures. For instance, the system dynamically calculates and displays a 'ranking' of the alternatives (see Figure 8.8) based on single criterion (e.g. the criterion experience) or on an aggregation of all the criteria using a mathematical method which takes into account the information expressed by the users about their preference structures (criteria weights, 'feasibility' intervals, aspiration levels, etc.).

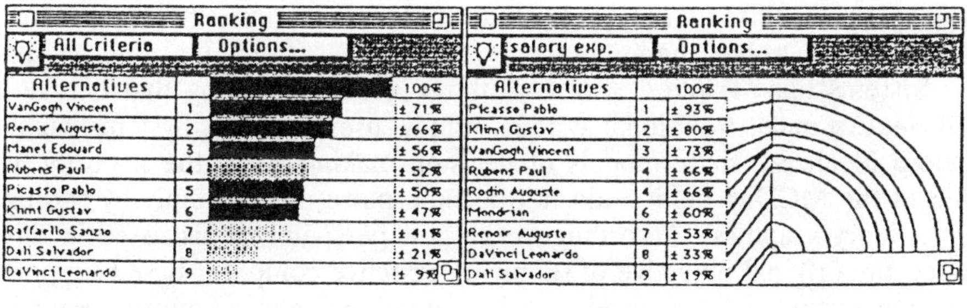

Fig. 8.8 Rankings: one of the analysis-supporting tools of 'Triple C'.

Each modification of these parameters will cause the system to update the ranking allowing the decision maker to evaluate visually the impact of the different criteria on a 'rational' ranking of the alternatives (see Angehrn (1990) for a more detailed description of the MCDM models used in this context).

Equally important is that the decision maker is not obliged to accept the rankings proposed by the system. The major aim of using a mathematical method for generating such a ranking is not to deliver 'optimal solutions'. The method plays here more the role of a 'rational myth' which stimulates the users to understand and express their preferences. In fact, the decision maker can modify the rankings computed by the system by simply moving and permuting the lines of the suggested ranking (each line corresponding to an alternative). Such a permutation implicitly corresponds to the specification of a different order between some of the alternatives. As a feedback, 'Triple C' will then dynamically suggest a new weighting of the criteria. The new weights − calculated by a quadratic optimization method and visually displayed in a tool such as the one in Figure 8.7 − will reflect the changes performed on the ranking by the decision maker and support the analysis of the relationships between the alternatives.

8.6 CONCLUSIONS

As anticipated in the introduction section, the alternative support perspective and the design guidelines proposed in this paper lead to a different kind of Decision Support Systems (symbiotic/convivial systems as described in Illich's (1973) precognitions). The paramount characteristics of such new systems are (1) the high level of human-computer interaction achieved during a decision-making process, and (2) their objective of supporting users to better understand and communicate their decisions rather than to 'solve' them.

Systems like 'Triple C' can contribute in demonstrating that it is not sufficient to make traditional systems simply 'user-friendly'. Systems which impose idealized, static models of decision making − as the majority of DSS in the MCDM field − do not become more useful simply by adding some 'fancy graphics'. According to the new perspectives discussed in this paper, the original objective of supplying effective computer-based support for non-routine, ill-structured decision situations requires more research effort in order to:

a. understand better the different dimensions of system flexibility needed to enhance intuition and creativity along individual, dynamic learning processes;

b. develop concepts and means such as Visual Interaction, which open new ways of man-machine cooperation in problem solving and decision making; and

c. guide DSS designers to move from the traditional 'solving- oriented' perspective of delivering decision support to an 'insights-' and 'communication-oriented' perspective, which take into account that decisions are always "someone's decisions".

REFERENCES

Alter, S. (1977) A taxonomy of decision support systems, *Sloan Management Review,* 19, 1.

Angehrn, A.A. (1989) Modeling by example: new ideas for interactive decision support. Paper presented at the Sixth EURO Summer Institute on DSS, Madeira, Portugal, May-June 1989; forthcoming in *European Journal of Operational Research.*

Angehrn, A.A. (1990) 'Triple C': a visual interactive MCDSS, INSEAD Working Paper.

Angehrn, A.A. and Luthi, H., (1990) Visual interactive modeling & intelligent dss: putting theory into practice, in: *DSS-90 Transactions,* Cambridge, MA. Forthcoming in *Interfaces.*

Bell, P.C., Parker, D.C. and Kirkpatrick, P. (1984) Visual interactive problem solving − a new look at management problems, Business Quarterly, Spring.

Bui, T.X. and Jarke, M. (1985) A decision support system for cooperative multiple criteria decision making, in Proc. of the 6th Int. Conf. on Information Systems, Tucson.

Chang, S. (1987) Visual languages: a tutorial and survey, in *Visualization in Programming,* P. Gorny and K.J. Tauber (eds), Lect. Notes in Comp. Science, Vol. 282, Springer-Verlag, Berlin.

Checkland, P. (1985) From optimizing to learning: a development of system thinking for the 1990s, *Journal of the Operational Research Society,* 36, 9.

Courbon, J.C. (1984) Transparency of data, information and models in *Decision Support Systems, Operational Research '84,* J.P. Brans (ed.), Elsevier Science Publishers.

Edwards, W. and Newman, J.R. (1982) *Multiattribute Evaluation,* Sage, Beverly Hills, CA.

Eom, H.B. (1989) The current state of multiple criteria decision support systems, *Human Systems Management,* 8.

Geoffrion, A.M. (1989) Computer-based modeling environments, *European Journal of Operational Research,* 41.

Illich, I. (1973) *Tools for Conviviality,* Perennial Library, Harper & Row, New York.

Jarke, M., Jelassi, M.T. and Shakun, M.F. (1987) Mediator: towards a negotiation support system, *European Journal of Operational Research,* 31.

Jelassi, M.T., Jarke, M. and Stohr, E.A. (1985) Designing a generalized multiple criteria decision support system, *Journal of Management Information Systems*, 1, 4.

Jones, C.V. (1989) An introduction to graph-based modeling systems. Working Paper 89-11-03, Department of Decision Sciences, The Wharton School, University of Pennsylvania.

Keen, P.G.W. (1987) DSS: the next decade, decision support systems, *The Int. Journal*, 3, 3.

Keen, P.G.W. and Scott Morton, M.S. (1978) *Decision Support Systems: An Organizational Perspective*, Addison-Wesley, Reading, MA.

Keeney, R.L. and Raiffa, H. (1976) *Decisions with Multiple Objectives*, John Wiley, New York.

Norman, D. and Draper, S. (1986) *User Centered System Design, New Perspectives on Human-Computer Interaction*, LEA Publishers.

Roy, B. (1971) Problems and methods with multiple objective functions, *Mathematical Programming*, 1.

Saaty, T.L. (1986) Axiomatic foundation of the analytic hierarchy process, *Management Science*, 32, 7.

Schneiderman, B. (1987) *Designing the User Interface: Strategies for Effective Human-Computer Interaction*, Addison-Wesley, Reading, MA.

Simon, H. (1960) *The New Science of Management Decision*, Harper & Row, New York.

Smith, C., Irby, C., Kimball, R., Verplank, B. and Harslem, E. (1982) designing the Star user interface, *BYTE*, 7, 4.

Sprague, R.H. Jr. and Watson, H.J. (1989) *Decision Support Systems: Putting Theory into Practice*, Prentice-Hall International Editions.

Stefick, M., Bobrow, D.G., Foster, G., Lanning, S. and Tartar, D. (1987) WYSIWIS revised: early experiences with multiuser interfaces, *ACM Transactions Office Inf. Systems*, 5, 2.

Turban, E. (1988) *Decision Support and Expert Systems*, Macmillan, New York.

Turban, E. and Carlson, J.G. (1989) Interactive visual decision making, in Sprague and Watson (1989).

Winograd, T. and Flores, F. (1986) Understanding Computers and Cognition: A New Foundation for Design, Ablex.

Zeleny, M. (1982) *Multiple Criteria Decision Making*, McGraw-Hill, New York.

Zeleny, M. (1989) Cognitive equilibrium: a new paradigm of decision making? *Human Systems Management,* 8.

Part Five

Case Studies

9 Cyberfilter:
a management support system

R. Espejo
Aston University, Birmingham

9.1 INTRODUCTION

This paper updates and develops further the paper 'A Tool for Distributed Planning', presented to the Orwellian Symposium and International Conference on Systems Research, Information and Cybernetics held in Baden-Baden, Germany, 1984 by the present author and Osvaldo Garcia.

This paper reports on recent work in the design and implementation of Cyberfilter, a management support system. This system is based on management cybernetics, in particular on ideas about the management of complexity (Ashby 1964; Beer 1975, 1979, 1981, 1985; Espejo and Watt 1979; Espejo 1979, 1980).

This application attempts to improve the performance of managers by designing the matching of their limited information processing capacity against the larger complexity of their relevant organizational tasks. Ashby's law of Requisite Variety makes apparent that this matching takes place at one level of performance or another; 'only variety absorbs variety' (Ashby 1964). If left to chance it may well be that the limited variety of the manager is mostly absorbed by irrelevant data, while truly important data (from the viewpoint of the manager him/herself) is left unattended. Indeed, because of the ill-structured nature of most managerial activities, this proposition is not trivially apparent. However, if we agree that managers can do better than that allowed by chance, then it makes sense to engineer the matching in question: it should increase the likelihood of higher levels of performance.

This paper offers one particular application of variety engineering; that of filtering relevant managerial information from the wealth of organizational data. The application in itself is not new; Cyberfilter was originally discussed by Beer (1979); however today's extraordinary developments in information technology permit us to implement much more effective designs.

The first part of the paper elaborates on Cyberfilter as a Management Support System (MSS): this part is followed by a model of the manager-task interaction. This model triggers methodological questions, in particular, about the measurement of performance. Indeed measurement is a highly specialized topic — in many ways beyond the scope of this paper and though the use of Cyberfilter, by and large, relies on standard accounting procedures, the third part of this paper discusses a very general measurement system which is responsible for the versatility of Cyberfilter. The final parts of the paper discuss the user's interface with Cyberfilter and the coupling of this system to other data processing systems in the organization.

9.2   MEANING OF CYBERFILTER

From the viewpoint of a manager, Cyberfilter is a computer aid that both attenuates the complexity of the world, by using aggregated data and by filtering out irrelevant data, and amplifies the manager's appreciation of that complexity, by supporting the structuring of richer mental models.

The effect in managers of this balanced development of attenuation and amplification is more effective models of action. At the same time that, because of filtration, they are bombarded by fewer irrelevant data, they are able to develop more complex cognitive models, because of synchronized reporting, by discovering relationships between essential variables (something which makes their relevant world simpler, more transparent).

Managers should find, as they improve their performance, that it pays to learn about organizational situations through these models. The implication of more effective mental models, from the viewpoint of information processing, is to permit a distancing of the manager from the tasks of his/her concern without losing control; that is, to make viable a larger information gap. Better models tip the balance between local and distant information in favour of the latter. There is no need for the manager to get involved in the details of everything in progress, he/she can rely on the monitoring of essential variables and therefore get more time to become involved with the less clear, unstructured aspects of his/her job (Figure 9.1).

From the perspective of Beer's work (Beer 1979, Chapter 11) the meaning of Cyberfilter is that of a 'box' recording, updating ... relevant criteria of stability (policies, plans, options and expectations) and a 'meter' measuring from a manager's point of view the stability or instability of the variables defining the performance of organizational tasks vis-à-vis their environments (Figure 9.2).

While interactions between the organization and its environment take place at several structural levels, the content of these interactions depends upon the distribution of discretion in the organization. The meaning of stability in these relations could be defined by general or functional managers, as was implied above, or by a group of managers controlling an organizational task.

For instance if the relevant viewpoint were corporate managers with functional discretion in financial, marketing and personnel matters, Cyberfilter will be looking at stability − between the company and the (tacitly defined) relevant environment − along these three dimensions. If Cyberfilter were in use by only one of the managers (or by each of them independently), say by the finance manager, concern would be the financial stability of the company. In all cases the point is that Cyberfilter can help managers to monitor the required stability of the activities they are accountable for with their environments.

In this paper we develop the first viewpoint; that is, the viewpoint of a particular manager for whom, as suggested earlier, Cyberfilter is an aid both to filter out situational complexity and to amplify his/her managerial capacity.

The main reason for choosing this viewpoint is to make apparent that Cyberfilter is relevant to all managers/supervisors in an organization, independent of their structural level in the organization or of their functional responsibilities.

Our view is that, as a matter of fact, if both the attenuation and amplification − between a manager and the situations of his/her concern − are done more effectively, then we can expect, because of Ashby's law, a higher managerial performance.

9.3   PRIMARY ACTIVITIES

The scope of Cyberfilter is the managerial control of an organization's 'primary activity'.

Primary activities are the tasks producing, at different levels of aggregation, the services or products that the organization is offering to its external clients. Cyberfilter is intended to support the managerial control of these activities. Hence, Cyberfilter is not an aid to control the organization's internal processes. It is intended to support the control of the organizational tasks, vis-à-vis the environment, at several levels of aggregation.

At the most aggregated level the total organization is a primary activity; it is offering products or services to customers. Next, the divisions in charge of producing types of services or products are the second level of primary activities. And indeed, most likely, specific products or services will be primary activities at a third level and so forth. This is referred to as the 'unfolding of organizational complexity' (Espejo 1983).

What is common to all primary activities is that their outputs are focused in the organization's environment and that they have their own management. What is likely to be different from one primary activity to another is the key variables that managers perceive they need to keep under control. For instance, in local government, a local authority is a primary activity in its own right. Within it 'housing' and 'technical services' could be primary activities at a second level, and within technical services, 'building control', 'development control' and 'transport and refuse collection' could be primary activities at a third level. Finally, within each of the services, any set of autonomous units responsible for the delivery of the services could be defined as the fourth level of primary activities.

In industry, while the 'company' is certainly a first level, the 'product divisions' could be the second, and the 'plants' and 'sections' could respectively be the third and fourth levels of primary activities. Cyberfilter aims at supporting the control of performance at all these levels.

9.4   A MANAGEMENT CONTROL MODEL

Our purpose in discussing a management control model is to clarify a few relevant methodological points. From the viewpoint of complexity managers are responsible for the regulation and control of tasks which produce far more complexity than they themselves can deal with; that is, they cannot match one-to-one the states of the systems they are accountable for. Two systemic implications emerge from this fact:

1. First, managers cannot possibly know all that is going on in the systems under their attention. They manage systems that are, as a matter of fact, opaque to them: an information gap, between what is going on and what they know, is inherent to management. If they are not going to be consumed by the details of local situations and therefore deny for themselves a comprehensive picture of the whole, they are forced to keep a distance from the systems. Managers cannot see in all detail the processes inside the 'black boxes' they manage; for control purposes they have to rely, by and large, on monitoring their outputs and controlling some of their inputs. This is a fact; what may vary from manager to manager is their distance to the black box: if they are too close the likelihood is that they will inhibit performance within the box, as people wait for instructions to undertake any action; if they are too distant the likelihood is that they will not know which levers to use to steer the box in a desirable direction (Espejo 1983).

2. Second, since the complexity of management situations is exceedingly large, no doubt, they are appreciated from multiple, equally valid,

viewpoints; managers develop, and constantly work out, new mental constructs of these situations. Tacitly, by choosing to look at a set of particular variables they are naming the systems relevant to their purposes. Methodologically, the boundaries of these systems are defined by the organizational variables managers perceive should be monitored and controlled in any particular situation. Indeed, it is not uncommon that these constructs are vague, inconsistent, incompatible. In any case, managers are always working out new constructs, that is, naming new systems, in parallel with changes in their appreciations.

The above systemic considerations permit us structuring, from the viewpoint of a particular manager, a simple control model: this model is described in Figure 9.3. A manager names — tacitly — the system that he/she perceives is accountable for. If the manager is a general manager the named system is likely to be a primary activity as a whole, however if he/she is a functional manager the named system is likely to be a functional slice of the related primary activity. The performance of this system is defined by the performance of the variables he/she finds necessary to monitor (this is the output of the — tacitly — named system). Performance of the system depends upon the response strategies that the manager can produce to correct errors or to anticipate the effects of environmental disturbances (threats and/or opportunities). Producing responses depends upon the variables the manager perceives he/she can control (controllable variables). Whether performance is adequate or not depends upon expectations; that is, upon the results the manager perceives as necessary for the monitored variables.

From the viewpoint of an information analyst, the above model permits the definition of basic activities necessary to develop a management support system (Figure 9.4):

3. Naming the system: if the main criterion in designing the information system is the need to produce 'pragmatic information' for the manager, that is, information that he/she can act upon, then the analyst needs to elicit both the transformations (from inputs to outputs) that the manager perceives he/she is accountable for, and the basic assumptions underlying these transformations, particularly those assumptions about the contribution, attitudes, possibilities, values ... of participants. Indeed a manager may be asked to name more than one system, to iterate several times before he/she is satisfied that 'those' are the transformations he/she is aiming at. To support the process of naming systems the analyst may use special techniques like root definitions (Checkland 1981) or task definitions (Espejo 1989).

4. Defining performance factors: naming the system permits the definition of monitored, controllable and non-controllable variables. The first set are the performance variables; the manager regulates them by 'pulling the strings' attached to the controllable variables. Indeed, not all levels of performance are acceptable, hence the manager operates with reference to a set of explicit, or tacitly held, performance values; these are the systemic behaviours that give stability to the manager. They may be referred to, simplistically, as the goals, objectives of the manager. No one is better than the manager him/herself, to define the critical factors impinging upon the performance of the monitored variables. These managerially defined performance factors reflect the manager's appreciation of the system's environment, its internal structure and human relations. These factors, in the manager's judgement, are critical to achieve required performance. These factors can be anticipatory or remedial. Indeed the whole idea is regulating performance, as far as possible, by anticipating problems, and not by error detection, though in the end both are always present.

Critical Success Factors (CSF) as defined by Rockart (1979) are, in my view, a special case of performance factors; this is the case when the manager is the chief executive of the firm and the system is the whole organization as perceived by that executive.

5. Measurement: the fact that the manager cannot have full knowledge of the system he/she is accountable for, that is, the fact that he/she cannot experience all systemic states, makes measurement a necessity. Measurement makes possible knowing about systems and their variations without diving into the systems or experiencing those variations. 'Measurement is the matching of one aspect of one domain to an aspect of another' (Stevens 1968).

The information analyst faces the problem of defining measures that are both useful descriptors of variations in the system, and relevant to the regulatory purposes of the manager. While the actual forms of measurement will depend, by and large, upon conventional accounting methods, no doubt there is room for creative forms of measurement. Whatever the measures are they should have the properties of 'validity', that is, of measuring what they are supposed to measure, of 'sensitivity', that is, of discriminating along the dimensions of concern and of 'reliability', that is, of replicability.

6. Data processing and reporting: the very process of recording data implies a form of measurement, that is, implies the matching of one aspect of the managerial situation of concern to a record in a 'file'. Of course raw data in general is managerially irrelevant; it brings the manager too close to the 'black box'. Hence, measurement in general

implies substantial data processing. Procedures to aggregate and filter data over time, as well as procedures for an opportune reporting are fundamental to management information. Indeed it is not good enough to increase by orders of magnitude the data processing and reporting capabilities of an organization if there is not human matching to make use of the recorded data. Data proliferation can be as damaging to the performance of a manager as the lack of relevant data. This is an increasingly important issue, both from the managerial and economic viewpoints. The design of Cyberfilter addresses this issue.

9.5 A SYSTEM FOR MEASUREMENT

9.5.1 Definition of indices

Cyberfilter is designed to use one particular system of measurement; however, this system is based on the wide range of measures of performance normally used in organizations. All organizations have, in one form or another, a measurement system, if sophisticated and well developed the easier should be the implementation of Cyberfilter. On the other hand, if rudimentary it should give the chance of developing new, more exciting performance measures.

This system of measurement was developed by Beer (1981) and has been used in a wide range of situations beyond its original application to production control. The three building blocks of the measurement system are the concepts of actuality, capability and potentiality. Actuality is the current value of the measured variable, capability is the best possible value that the variable can take, accepting present levels of resources and organizational constraints, and potentiality is the value the variable ought to take if constraints are removed and resources developed. From them, as can be seen in Figure 9.5, it is possible to derive three indices:

1. Productivity or the index of achievement is the ratio between actuality and capability — if better means more (e.g. production per day), or is the ratio between capability and actuality if better means less (e.g. hours necessary to do a job). This way the value of all indices can vary only from 0 to 1, and in all cases the closer the value is to 1 the higher is the achievement. Since in most of the economics literature productivity is understood as an 'input/output' ratio, Beer's index of productivity is being renamed as the index of achievement.

2. Latency is the ratio between capability and potentiality, or the other way round, depending upon the scalar order of potentiality and capability. In any case this index also varies between 0 and 1 and the

closer it is to 1 the more the system is using its latent resources. This index is a measure of possible developments into the future based on current activities, since the first block in this measurement system is an actuality. In other words the index of latency measures how far the system can go by removing constraints and allocating resources, that is, by increasing its capabilities.

3. Performance is defined both as the ratio between actuality and potentiality (or the other way round depending upon their scalar order) or the product of the indices of achievement and latency. Again, it can vary only from 0 to 1, and the closer it is to 1 the better the performance is. However a value close to 1 suggests that that variable, from the viewpoint of the manager, no longer has potential for growth. The meaning of performance is meshing present and future by measuring the balance between the all too natural drive for short term achievements and the need to develop resources to maintain or increase achievements in the future. It is a managerial illusion to believe that a high index of achievement is good in itself; if that achievement implies running down the available resources, that is, pushing down the capability, poor long term achievements are likely to bring home the shortsighted nature of this management. The index of performance helps to make apparent such an effect now; as achievement goes up, performance may well go down.

The scope of applicability of this system of measurement is large; among other applications it gives a powerful reference to discuss problems of production at the shopfloor level as well as problems of organizational development at the corporate level. For production the actuality may well be the number of units produced per day, for organizational development the actuality may be the current quality of organizational communications, possibly using an ordinal scale of measurement. In both cases it should be possible, for those directly related to the situations, to think about meaningful references of improved achievements (capabilities). However, in general, the definition of capabilities should be the outcome of organizational audits and not of unilateral definitions by the affected manager.

Since Cyberfilter assumes that the manager wants a stable behaviour of the monitored variables, that is, wants to keep them under control, it is expected that the manager will interfere with their trends as long as these are considered undesirable. In Churchman's terms (Churchman 1971), our system of measurement is of the kind 'integrated past and future', that is, Cyberfilter assumes the manager is closing a loop which integrates his/her past learning, his/her present action and the expected future behaviour of the monitored 'variable' in the form of a feed-forward mechanism; the instability that was to happen but never did ... type of situation, that is, the action of a manager that averted a foreseen instability.

The unfolding of complexity in organizations says that this 'manager-variable' balance happens at all structural levels. This fact is not always recognized, perhaps because there is the belief that management is mainly done at higher structural levels, and not at all levels, from minding machines to corporate control. Multiple organizational problems derive from underdeveloped control loops, just because managers feel constrained in their initiatives. Under-developed loops produce poor distributed control in the organization and multiple instabilities.

Implicit to Cyberfilter is the idea of matching the unfolding of organizational complexity — the *de facto* organizational distribution of discretion/autonomy to make possible the control of its task — to measures of performance (the indices). These measures are tools for performance control at all structural levels. Moreover, if this design included a concern for organizational effectiveness we would not be accepting the *de facto* situation, but we would be suggesting improvements to the unfolding of complexity by design. However, consistent with the chosen viewpoint we can say only that, whether the manager of concern realizes it or not, he/she is constrained by an organisational structure, and that a matching of the level of aggregation in the monitoring variables implied by his/her *de facto* position in the structure to the level of aggregation he/she chooses to monitor is likely to improve individual and organizational performance. This in itself is a measurement problem!

9.6   CYBERFILTER

9.6.1 User's interface

If the 'manager-variable loop' is effective the behaviour of indices should be stable, that is, the actuality should be expected to fluctuate around a stable value. Figure 9.6 is a typical time-series, which in spite of its several changes in level of achievement and in spite of the multiple transients, shows stability around three stable values. Indeed, Figure 9.6 may be a case in which the effectiveness of the 'manager-variable loop' can be improved. Index stability assumes:

1. The manager sees a purpose in maintaining the stability of the variable. This should be the case if the 'named system' is still relevant to the manager.

2. The manager has the levers to control the behaviour of the variable and knows (learns) how to use them! That is, if his/her assumptions prove

to be correct. Indeed, organizational conflicts and environmental changes may render a previously controllable situation, uncontrollable.

3. The measurement has the properties of validity, sensitivity and reliability. It is not uncommon that a measure does not measure what it is intended to measure, in which case there is no reason to expect a stable behaviour!

Of course, as Figure 9.6 makes apparent, stable does not mean static. Over time significant changes in the behaviour of the variable should not only be expected but also planned. Cyberfilter helps both in alerting managers about likely changes and in planning the desirable changes. The technical aspects of the statistical analysis in Cyberfilter have been discussed before by Beer (1979): for the purposes of this paper it should suffice to point out that Cyberfilter uses Bayesian statistical theory according to the protocol developed by Harrison and Stevens (1971).

The following discussion explains the capabilities of Cyberfilter from the viewpoint of the manager-user:

4. In general, we may expect, if the manager is to maintain a reasonable distance from the 'black box' that about seven indices (the magic number 7±2) should be enough to monitor the system's performance. Indeed, it is not the independent behaviour of indices, but their dynamic interrelations in time, that recreates, in the manager's mind − to an extent − the complexity of the real world, thus permitting a richer managerial appreciation of the situational complexity. In practice, since managers are used to receive large quantities of data, they may perceive the need for a larger number of indices. This may imply, paradoxically, reducing the manager's span of control, simply because more indices not only put the manager closer to the 'black box' but increase the dimensions of control, something which inhibits the initiative of the people operating within the 'black box', thus making the box smaller in complexity. No doubt psychological aspects like cognitive style and the ability to accept uncertainty, differentiate managers from managers, and in the end the 'right' number of indices is idiosyncratic to each manager, though managerial learning should alter this number over time.

5. At any time an index can be in any of the following seven states:

*   STABLE if the current value is fluctuating around a stable value, which is equal to the current statistical mean value of the time series.
*   TRANSIENT if the current value is abnormal, but the likelihood is that the next value will be normal.
*   UNSTABLE if the current value is in a succession of transient values. That is, if the uncertainty of the state of the 'next' value in a succession of values is high.

- DECREASING if the current value is on a downward slope. This state is particularly relevant since it indicates an incipient instability in the behaviour of the index while the mean value still remains the same. This state alerts the manager about likely changes in the mean value. This state permits recognizing presymptoms.
- INCREASING if the current value is in an upward slope. The meaning of this state is the same as the previous one.
- UP if the current value is stable at a higher mean value than that of recent history. The current mean value of the index is higher than the recent mean value.
- DOWN if the current value is stable at a lower stability value. The current mean value of the time series is lower than the recent mean value.

Asterisks are used to mark the states where there is a (perhaps) managerially significant change in the behaviour of the index and therefore reporting might be necessary: Cyberfilter can establish the likelihood of such changes before they take place, hence making it possible for the manager to influence the future. Most of the above states are illustrated in the stability graph of Figure 9.7. This graph is the summary of Cyberfilter reports for the time series of Figure 9.6.

If exceptions are reported Cyberfilter helps the manager to examine the situation. The manager may enquire about the definition of the index, the filtered historical information in the form of the stability graphs (Figure 9.7), the exception reports for all indices (Figure 9.8), and also the assumptions underlying the accepted stability values. While this information may trigger enquiries for extra information, it may also lead to immediate action.

The manager has the option to control the rate of exceptions reported by controlling the position of a tuning 'knob' which alters the sensitivity of the statistical filtration, from positions of high sensitivity to positions of very slow response. For instance, if the manager thinks that too many exceptions are being reported he/she can adjust Cyberfilter by adjusting the knob to a slower response position. This adjustment or tuning is not trivial; it does not only imply changes in multiple statistical parameters but also in the balance manager-variable, that is, in the concept of stability. Nobody better than the manager to carry out these adjustments.

However, a major strength of Cyberfilter is the support it can give to distributed planning. This capability springs out of the measurement system in use. Related to the concepts of actuality, capability and potentiality, three forms of planning emerge (Figure 9.9):

6. Tactical planning: since Cyberfilter maintains an updated mean value for each of the essential variables it makes sense for the manager to use the short-term forecast as the plan for the short term. However, this planning becomes more significant when the manager's planned value is different to the anticipated statistical 'mean value' of the index. In this case, for planning to be meaningful the manager must take action; if nothing is done results may not match expectations.

7. Strategic planning: in general the value of the achievement index is short of its best possible value (i.e. 1), or in other words, there is a gap between actuality and capability. Since capability is the best realistic value that an essential variable can take, it makes sense to try to understand the reasons for the gap. Cyberfilter asks the manager for the assumptions made in defining the current value of capability, and his/her views about the current gap (these are called the annotations of achievement, which are kept in notes for inspection). The manager has the options of challenging the value of capability as well as of deciding new response strategies to improve achievement. An effective use of these options imply, in general, organizational negotiations. Capability is a systemic concept; changes in the capability of one variable, for instance reductions in the sales capability of an organization, are likely to assume changes in the capabilities of other organizational variables, for instance, in the production capabilities of that company.

8. Normative planning: again the manager interacts with Cyberfilter to make explicit the assumptions made in defining the current value of potentiality and the comments he/she has on current events hindering or facilitating the development of latent resources; these are the annotations of latency. In general they take the form of notes about investment plans, structural changes, technological innovations. The manager has the option to alter the value of potentiality but, of course, not before he/she has carried out adequate negotiations and secured the necessary commitments.

9.6.2 The system

On the technical front Cyberfilter is not new, its basic filtering concept is more than 30 years old (Beer 1966), yet its capability as a management tool has increased with recent information technology, in particular with the introduction of microcomputers in almost all activities. Cyberfilter has been implemented for IBM and compatible machines with high-resolution graphics capabilities (Syncho 1990). It can interface with other data-processing software either resident in mainframes or in the same workstation.

Figures 9.10 and 9.11 should help in understanding the coupling of Cyberfilter to the standard accounting procedures of an organization. Figure 9.10 gives a simplified description of the traditional interface between a manager and data-processing systems: raw data input is structured and updated in a database, managers may query directly, or more likely receive periodic reports, from this database. Figure 9.11 describes data-processing from the viewpoint of Cyberfilter: while the manager is responsible for the definition of indices, the source to calculate actualities is the organizational database. These calculations may be done in any spreadsheet, like Lotus 123, where the necessary algorithms to do the calculations are defined. These calculations produce the inputs to Cyberfilter, which may be left in an intray, from where the software takes the actualities to update time series. If incipient instability is detected Cyberfilter users will receive alerts when they log into their workstations. Reporting is an on-going process: as soon as an index is formed, it is analysed and if necessary an alert is triggered.

A major challenge in using this system is whether managers will overcome their widely-held view that they control what they inspect, and that they need detailed information about the tasks under their responsibility. A positive answer to this challenge implies accepting to undergo a genuine learning process, in which the balance between local and distant information moves towards the latter.

The measurement system used by Cyberfilter is indeed a major strength, but it also poses the difficulty of assuming a model of organizations and management that is not widely held by managers; this is the cybernetic model in which autonomy is the key concept. The necessary shift in paradigm may take some time, but it is already occurring; the technology we now have permits thinking in better management of complexity; once this fact is appreciated the gate to this more powerful view of organizations and management will be open.

As made apparent in Figure 9.11 the role of Cyberfilter should lie between the data-processing systems, which are adequate to handle large volumes of organizational data, and the underdeveloped management reporting systems which, by and large, have been designed with no insight into management processes. Matching the limited information processing capacity of managers to reports that do not overload them is a task that implies not only an understanding of individual cognitive styles but also of the organizational information flows.

REFERENCES

Ashby, R. (1964) *An Introduction to Cybernetics,* Methuen, London.

Beer, S. (1959) *Cybernetics and Management,* English University Press, London.

Beer, S. (1966) *Decision and Control,* Wiley, Chichester, UK.

Beer, S. (1975) *Platform for Change,* Wiley, Chichester, UK.

Beer, S. (1979) *The Heart of Enterprise,* Wiley, Chichester, UK.

Beer, S. (1981) *Brain of the Firm* (2nd edition), Wiley, Chichester, UK.

Checkland, P. (1981) *Systems Thinking, Systems Practice,* Wiley, Chichester, UK.

Churchman, W. (1971) The past's future, in *Measurement for Management Decision* by R. Mason and E.B. Swanson(eds), 1981, Addison-Wesley, Philippines.

Espejo, R. (1979) Cybernetic filtration of management information, in *Aston Management Centre WPS No. 126.*

Espejo, R. (1980) Information and management: the cybernetics of a small company, in *The Information Systems Environment,* H. Lucas (ed.), North-Holland, Amsterdam.

Espejo, R. (1983) Management and information: the complementarity control-autonomy, in *Cybernetics and Systems: An International Journal,* 14: 85-102.

Espejo, R. (1989) A cybernetic methodology for problem solving, unpublished monograph, Aston Business School.

Espejo, R. and Watt J. (1979) Management information systems: a system for design, *Journal of Cybernetics,* 9: 259-283.

Ginzberg, M.W. (1982) *Decision Support Systems,* E.Reitman and Stohr (eds), North Holland, Amsterdam.

Harrison, P.J. and Stevens, C. (1971) A Bayesian approach to short term forecasting, *Operational Research Quarterly,* Vol. 22, No. 4.

Rockart, J.F. (1979) Chief executives define their own data needs, *Harvard Business Review,* 57(2): 81-93.

Stevens, S.S. (1968) Measurement, statistics, and the schemapiric view, *Science,* Vol. 161, No. 3844, 849-856.

Syncho (1990) *Cyberfilter Manual,* Syncho Ltd, Aston Science Park, Birmingham, UK.

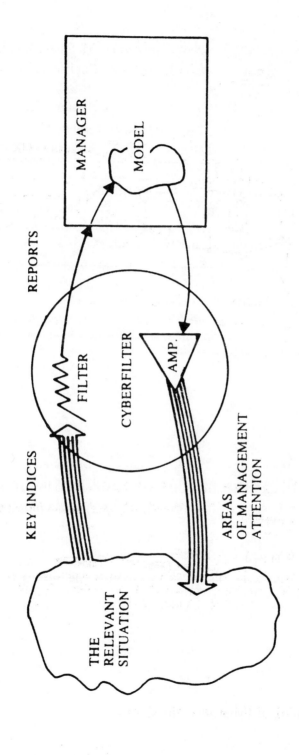

Fig. 9.1 Meaning of Cyberfilter attenuation and amplification.

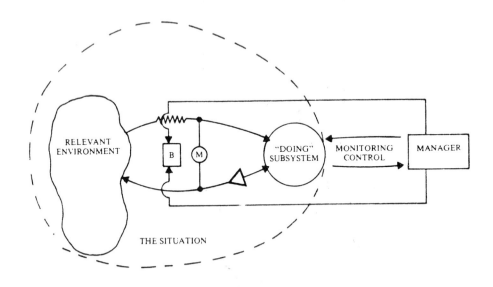

B: BOX WITH CRITERIA OF STABILITY AS DEFINED BY THE MANAGER

M: METER MEASURING THE STABILITY (WITH REFERENCE TO THE ABOVE CRITERIA)

CYBERFILTER: B + M

THE COMPLEXITY OF THE SITUATION IS ABSORBED TO A LARGE DEGREE BY THE DOING SUBSYSTEM, YET IT SHOULD BE UNDER THE MANAGER'S CONTROL: CYBERFILTER HELPS IN THIS.

Fig. 9.2 Meaning of Cyberfilter: the situation.

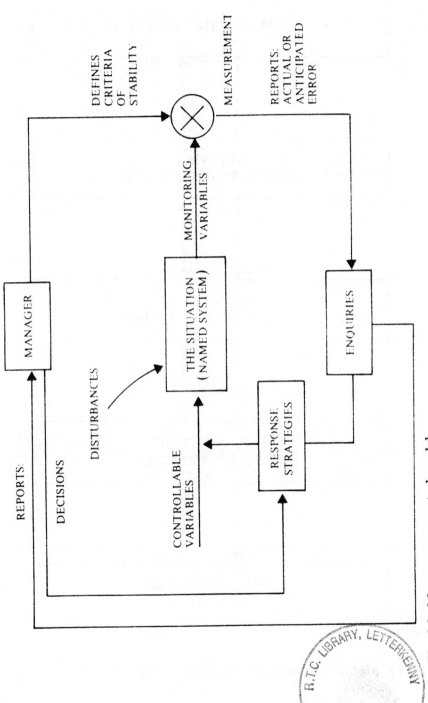

Fig. 9.3 Management control model.

DEFINES
CRITERIA
OF
STABILITY

MEASUREMENT

REPORTS:
ACTUAL OR
ANTICIPATED
ERROR

MONITORING
VARIABLES

MANAGER

THE SITUATION
(NAMED SYSTEM)

ENQUIRIES

DISTURBANCES

RESPONSE
STRATEGIES

CONTROLLABLE
VARIABLES

REPORTS:

DECISIONS

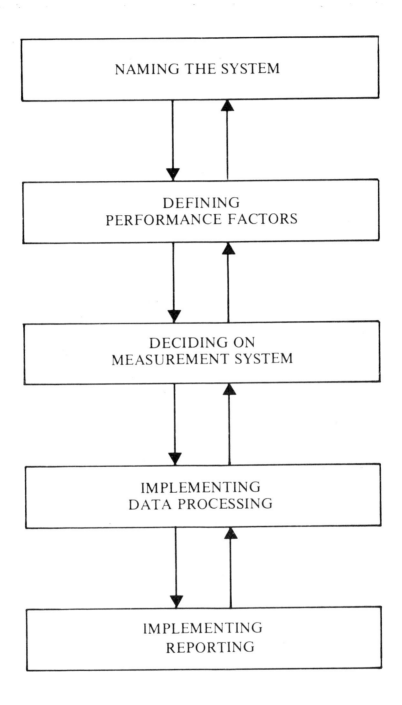

Fig. 9.4 Method to design control information systems.

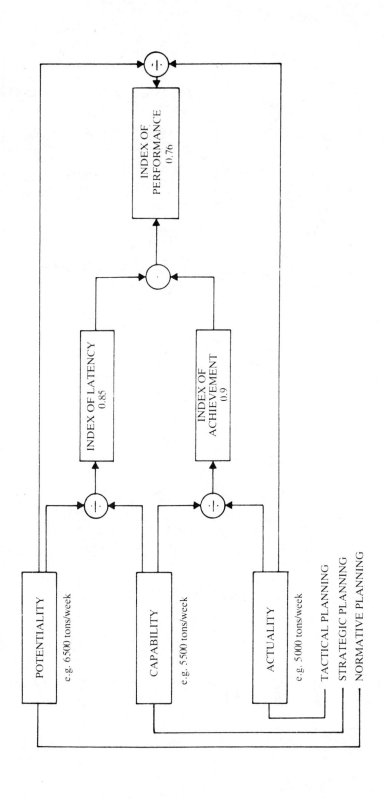

Fig. 9.5 Systems of measurement and planning.

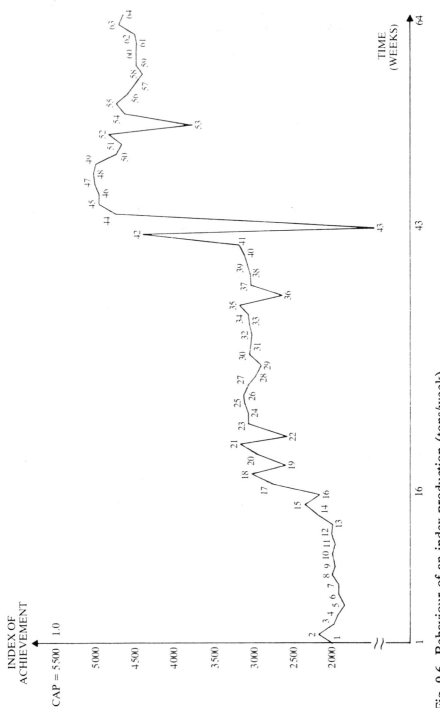

Fig. 9.6 Behaviour of an index production (tons/week).

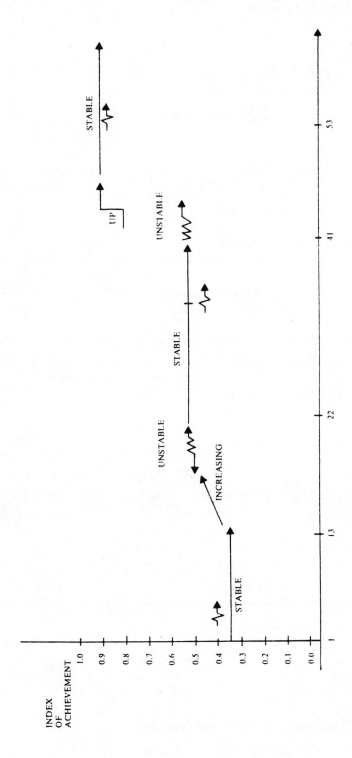

Fig. 9.7 Stability graph index of achievement production (tons/week).

DATE	INDEX	TYPE OF EXCEPTION
09/03/82	SALES	↘
15/03/82	OUTPUT VALUE	↘
21/04/82	MANUFACTURING PROD	⟶〜〜〜⟶
23/05/82	SALES	⌐_⟶
23/05/82	QUICK RATIO	↘
23/05/82	CURRENT RATIO	↘

Fig. 9.8 Exception reports all-indices.

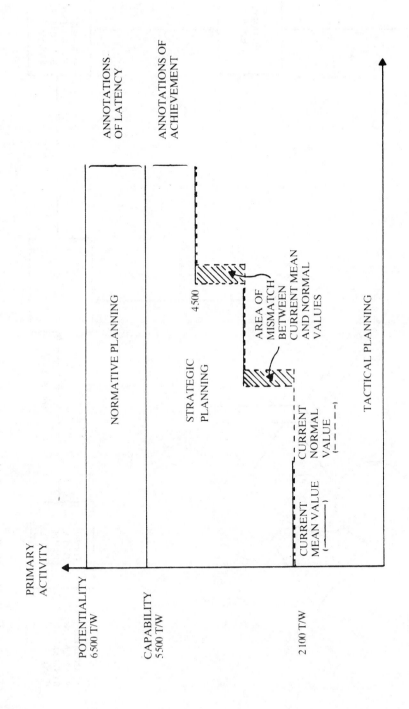

Fig. 9.9 Indices and planning: index of production.

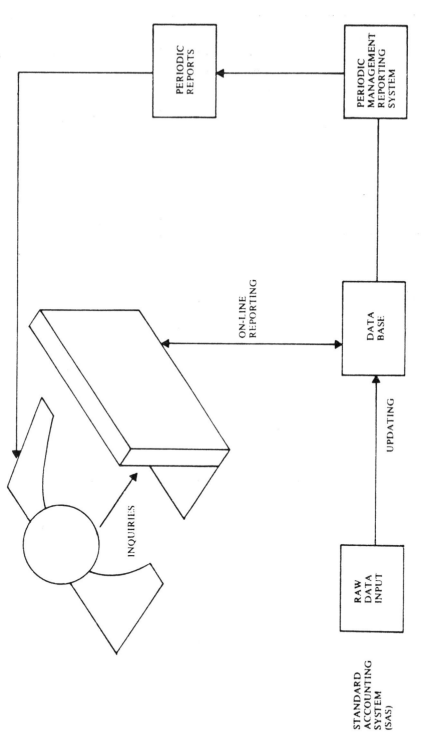

Fig. 9.10 Data processing and reporting standard accounting system.

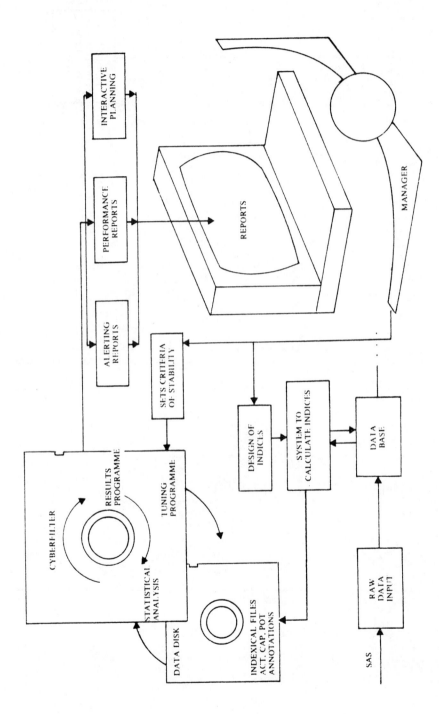

Fig. 9.11 Data processing and Cyberfilter.

10 EIS and total quality

Thoughts on the role of Information Systems in promoting corporate change

M. Callaghan
Head of Strategic Planning, London Underground Ltd

10.1 INTRODUCTION

The theme of this conference is the role of EIS and DSS in changing corporate cultures. London Underground has implemented EIS at a time of rapid organizational change, and the system has had to both drive, and respond to, the changes taking place. This has created an unrivalled opportunity to try and understand the role of information, and information systems, for senior managers.

My own involvement in this field is as a consultant with a professional interest in both organizational change and in information systems, and more specifically as one of the team responsible for London Underground's initial EIS development. It is only in the last few months, as a participant in the company's Quality Leadership Programme, that I have been introduced in any structured way to the principles of Total Quality. This paper is therefore more thinking out loud than the presentation of reasoned conclusions.

I should acknowledge that the presentation of the Total Quality ideas here is largely due to the originators of the Quality Leadership Programme, who include both the company's own staff and tutors from the PA Consulting Group.

Finally, I should say that the remarks here are aimed at two audiences. First, to the users of EIS — the senior managers, because defining information on corporate performance is, I think, more difficult than is often imagined. Second, to the systems providers. Not only do they have to implement quality systems, they also have a responsibility as information professionals to guide management in developing the specification they have to meet.

10.2 CORPORATE CHANGE IN LONDON UNDERGROUND

The main engine of change in London Underground at present is the Quality Leadership Programme — a series of training workshops, attended first by the top 300 managers, and due to be driven right through the management structure in 1991. This is the beginning of a thrust to embed the ideas of Total Quality Management (RQM) in the company.

Although the Total Quality initiative seeks to structure and codify new management principles, it is far from the beginning of London Underground's process of corporate change. The first major landmark was on 1 November 1988, when the management structure supporting the provision of train and station services was completely revised, and enormously strengthened. Now, every line is a separate business unit, with its own management team, under a general manager. Perhaps the greatest break with the past was the creation of the so-called 'Centurions'. These are middle managers directly responsible for a group of front-line staff — a concept unknown in the previous history of the company.

London Underground's involvement with EIS lies between the new organization structure and the introduction of Quality Leadership, both chronologically and conceptually. The intention to develop EIS was announced on 1 November 1988, at the same time as the reorganization. It was a technology completely new to London Underground, presenting information in a novel and accessible way. The intention was to reinforce the break with the past signalled by the management changes.

10.3 THE LESSONS OF TOTAL QUALITY

There seems to me clear resonances between many of the principles underlying Total Quality, and the concerns of those developing information systems to support senior management. I present these in the form of seven 'Total Quality Lessons'.

10.3.1 Total Quality is continually satisfying customers' agreed requirements

One of the fundamental themes of Total Quality is that everybody, whatever their role, is both a customer and a supplier, whether internal or external to the organization. Participants in Total Quality Programmes are therefore encouraged to develop a clear understanding of the customer-supplier chains to which they belong.

The concept of customer-supplier chains can be useful in determining key corporate information for inclusion in an EIS. Not only does it help in clarifying the measures which relate to the delivery of the final product to the external customer, it can be used to structure the drill-down, through each function or activity in the chain.

London Underground recently decided that one of its key measures would be the number of trains cancelled in each rush hour. The main reasons for cancellation are insufficient staff or serviceable stock. A possible drill-down through a related customer-supplier chain is shown in Figure 10.1. Note that this is independent of organization structure or hierarchy. Here the Personnel Director appears in the middle of the chain as a supplier to the Train Services Manager for the provision of recruits.

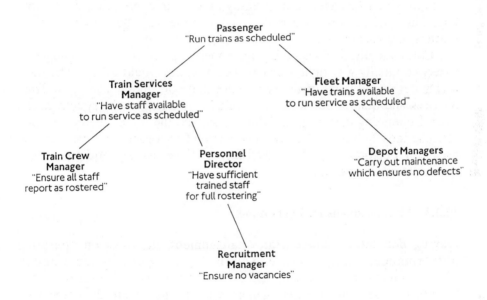

Fig. 10.1 Simplified customer-supplier chain.

The goal of continually satisfying customers' agreed requirements is, of course, one which applies to the providers of EIS systems themselves. We were set the task of developing an EIS to support the reorganization of LU in a little over three months, with no definition of the requirements, no skills in the technology and no people available. When the customer is the

Managing Director, the only view to take is that the project is ambitious but feasible, and so it proved.

It is important that in the definition of the customer-supplier relationship the goal is to satisfy agreed requirements. Often, the specification of requirements is a matter of negotiation, and this is true for the delivery of information systems. As a supplier, you shouldn't be too keen to accept the customers' definition of what they want. Users are often poor information analysts; more often, the suppliers have this skill, and are leading the users to a proper system definition.

10.3.2 You can't manage results, you can only manage processes

A common argument about EIS is that most senior executives are focused on the 'bottom line', so most systems have a financial orientation. The problem is that managers cannot easily have a direct effect on the bottom line. Financial performance is derived from the way the activities of the business are carried out.

Consequently, deciding to highlight operating performance, arguing that if service quality was right, financial performance would follow. The most highly developed parts of the system are therefore those relating to Train Services and Station Services. The Train Service part of the system covers overall operating performance information, and the initial analysis of train cancellations, failures and delays. The Station Service section covers lift and escalator performance, the availability of ticket-issuing equipment and queues at booking offices.

10.3.3 What getsmeasured gets done

Having decided to concentrate management attention on operating performance, what measures should be adopted? When London Under-ground came to develop EIS, we found that two measures of overall train service performance were generally used. These were the percentage of schedule operated, and the number of trains in peak service.

Percentage of schedule
The percentage of schedule measure is one which is used by BR and London Buses, as well as London Underground, and is the measure used by the Department of Transport in setting the so-called 'Quality of Service Targets' for these undertakings. Trains may be cancelled for mechanical, staff or operational reasons, or they may be re-routed or reversed short of their original destinations. All these actions cause fewer train miles to be run

than shown in the timetable or schedule, so 'percentage of schedule operated' has been taken as a global measure of the company's ability to keep cancellations and other disruptions to a minimum.

Two of the TQM messages raise question marks over this. Managers responsible for managing train service operations have pointed out that they have the ability to manipulate the service to increase their percentage of schedule, at the expense of making the service delivered to customers worse. For example, if the service were disrupted, and they were losing miles, managers on lines with more than one branch could route trains down the longer branch (which would increase mileage) and provide no service down the shorter. A true case of 'What gets measured gets done'.

Total quality is about continually satisfying agreed customer requirements. I wonder how many of those who are customers of the Underground (especially in central London rather than the suburbs) even know there is a timetable. Probably their requirement is more like 'provide a train to my destination every two minutes'. Remember the traditional bus stop complaint — 'I waited half an hour for a bus and then six came at once'. This isn't quality service, but it gives the same percentage of schedule operated as regular five-minute intervals.

One further point. The TQM message should make us question the data as well as the measure. It was only after we had implemented EIS that we found that the traditional way of calculating the percentage of schedule operated was to include empty stock moves — transfers of trains from one location to another for maintenance, for example. Achieving high scores on moving empty trains puts your performance up, but it doesn't do much for the customers. Now only 'loaded miles' (trains in passenger service) are counted.

Trains in peak service
The increased depth of managerial resources which was a feature of London Underground's reorganization in November 1988 has enabled the company to achieve some major successes, particularly in the relentless attention given to safety. Customers are unaware of much of this work, which is behind the scenes in machine rooms, depots and other areas unseen by the public. There is now scope to focus more management attention on the achievement of operating performance, which will make change visible. The measure being used to drive this focus is trains in peak service — simply the number of trains which enter service in each peak period (or rush-hour), compared with the number booked.

This measure does fall short of the ideal from the passengers' viewpoint. All the trains could run as booked, but without the even gaps which are part of the customers' specification, and without necessarily running to all destinations. Nevertheless, there is an argument that trains in peak service are a better proxy for the quality of service to customers than percentage of schedule. In the rush-hour, all lines run the maximum service that can be accommodated by the signalling. Therefore, if all the trains run as booked, the signalling itself will ensure roughly constant intervals through the central area.

The peak service measure also proved attractive for internal reasons. Apart from being simple and clearly measurable, the performance achieved is almost entirely within the control of each Line General Manager. The results of adopting it in June 1990 as a key driver of performance has been dramatic. The service on the Northern line today is better than at any time in the last 25 years, with zero cancellations frequently achieved. Similar results have occurred on the Bakerloo and Metropolitan lines. Across the network, cancellations are approaching our initial target of single figures (out of nearly 500 trains booked). The ultimate quality target is, of course, zero cancellations network-wide.

Whether or not it is the ideal customer-oriented measure, passengers have certainly felt the benefit of the motivational effects of setting this simple target.

Customer-driven measures
London Underground has monitored customer attitudes to its service for many years, and is continually developing its understanding of customers' expectations. So far, it has yet to establish better ways than those above of measuring day-to-day operational performance in a way which shows how well those expectations are being met. The TQM team is working with interested groups in the company to achieve this.

It may be that there is no single measure. The performance specification suggested earlier (a train to my destination every two minutes) only applies to high-frequency services such as those in the central area. Outside the central area, the problems are different. It is too expensive to run at this frequency. Where there are many branches, maybe only one train in three or four will be going to the further destinations. These are the conditions of a suburban commuter railway, not a mass-transit metro. Adherence to the published timetable is much more important, because customers rely on it more. Generally, organizations like to have consistent performance measures, to allow comparison between business units. Maybe, from the customers' perspective, this is wrong.

10.3.4 Ready, aim, fire

The syndrome of deciding on the solution before properly understanding the problem has been characterized as 'Ready, Fire, Aim'. London Underground, in creating its Quality Leadership programme, developed the Quality Wheel (Figure 10.2) as a mechanism for structuring the analysis of quality improvement opportunities. The idea of a 'Win-Win' is that well-chosen management action not only makes the organization more effective, but does it in a way which has a direct impact on the customer.

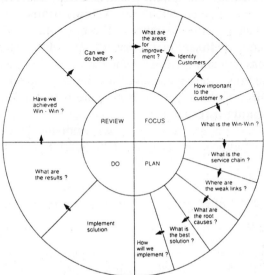

Fig. 10.2 The quality improvement diagram.

The planning stage is aimed at discovering root causes, because quality performance comes from understanding and dealing with causes, not symptoms. Heavy emphasis is given to determining causes in an analytical, data-driven way. Only solutions which can effectively be implemented are allowable, and the wheel is completed by a review process to ensure that the changes have been successful in improving performance.

A well-designed EIS ought to support organizational change based on an understanding of root causes. From the top level, customer-focused performance measures, the drill-down should take the user far enough through the customer-supplier chain to identify the likely reasons for poor performance. Underlying the EIS, there should be analytical tools and detailed data to help identify root causes. This is an important role of Decision Support systems. If these systems can model the effects of possible management intervention, so much the better.

A risk of EIS is that the drill-down and analytical tools will be inadequate. In these circumstances, the fact of poor performance may be exposed, so management feels that action is essential. Changes are then made by 'experience', guesswork or gut feel. The results are unpredictable, and are unlikely to represent sustained quality improvements.

10.3.5 Total quality means continuous improvement

This is another message for system providers. You will probably find that EIS users are dissatisfied with the system almost as soon as it is implemented. Changes will be sought in the way information is presented. There will be demands to add or change screens. More significantly, as the performance measures and the underlying data are more closely scrutinized and better understood, they themselves will be challenged.

The credibility of the system will be judged in the long term by the organization's ability to respond to these criticisms. This means that both the information providers (who are probably not the IT department) and the EIS technical support function, must be geared for swift and frequent change.

10.3.6 Obviously the obvious isn't so obvious, or more people would be doing it

So says quality guru Tom Peters. When challenged to think about the most basic propositions of Total Quality, our experience has been that nearly everyone resists at the start — 'We tried that once, it didn't work', 'We do it like that anyhow', 'That's not new — surely everyone does that', 'That's not the way we do things round here'. After a time, and some honest self-examination, doubts begin to set in.

This phenomenon can also be explained in terms of the five stages of grief:

Denial — 'Nobody can say that we don't care about quality.'
Anger — 'How dare you say we don't understand quality.'
Rationalization — 'Our industry is different, so TQM ideas don't really fit our circumstances.'
Acceptance — 'You're quite right — we don't do things in a quality way.'
Action — 'We're going to do things in a quality way.'

No matter how skilled or experienced as providers or users of information, I believe everyone can gain something from the lessons of Total Quality.

10.3.7 If you always do what you've always done, you'll always get what you've always got

Some people find it puzzling that EIS should be seen as a driver of organizational change. All it does is display information in a new way.

If this is its function, then the sceptics are right — it doesn't contribute to change. If the EIS is simply the next system off the DP manager's application production line, if the information it contains is the same as in the monthly briefing book, if senior managers don't focus on performance, if no debate is generated about the quality and usefulness of the system and the data it contains, then you're doing what you've always done, and you'll get what you've always got. There is a good chance that the system will be just a corporate toy.

The life-cycle of EIS in London Underground is nothing like this. In the early stages, managers became EIS users by invitation. Managers who asked for their terminal to go to a secretary or subordinate were told 'You take the system or not, as you choose, but you can't use substitutes.' They all took it. It identified them as part of the team.

Since then, there has been heavy demand to be an EIS user, to become 'part of the team'. At the same time, there have been high levels of dissatisfaction among the original user group about the measures displayed, the quality of the underlying data, the method of presentation, the timeliness of the information ...

This level of dissatisfaction seems to me healthy. Very few of the grievances are (if we look at root causes) about the system itself. Most are about whether the information available is 'right' — appropriate, accurate, timely — to enable senior management to achieve its performance goals.

As long as the debate is over issues like these, then the quality culture, with its demand for continuous improvement, is alive, and the 'win-win' is achievable — a better EIS, leading to a better service for customers.

11 EIS evolution at British Airways

A. Popovich
British Airways

11.1 OBJECTIVES OF PAPER

The objectives of this paper are as follows:
- To analyse the evolution of the AIMS first-generation EIS from initial enthusiasm to maturity.
- To analyse the approach adopted so far in developing and promoting the MERLIN second-generation EIS, targeted for release in March 1991.
- To identify issues and pitfalls faced by implementing EIS based on the AIMS and MERLIN experience.

11.2 FIRST-GENERATION EIS: THE AIMS SYSTEM

11.2.1 History and marketing

AIMS (Airline Information Management System) is a mainframe-based system developed in-house in the APL programming language to run on a VM mainframe. The AIMS system went live in September 1983 for fifteen executive users.

Initial attempts at Marketing Aims prior to 1983 suffered from an inability to persuade a longstanding generation of executives who questioned the added value of an EIS for their own style of running the business. At the same time, they were fully aware of increasing difficulties arising from a recession in the airline industry.

It was only after the appointment of John King in 1981 to the chairmanship of British Airways and two years later of Colin Marshall to the post of Chief Executive, that there was a move to change the way the organization did business by focusing its culture and management style on customer service. Shortly after joining British Airways, Marshall brought in a senior consultant Mike Levin to assist him in transforming management values. Levin soon saw the potential of the AIMS initiative which was still struggling to gain a foothold within the executive community. As a result, from 1983 onwards the fortunes of the AIMS initiative improved dramatically.

11.2.2   Payback

Payback from the AIMS investment came from British Airways' ability to respond positively to the adverse impact on the airline industry of the Libya and Chernobyl incidents in 1986/1987. Despite there being a decline in US citizens' travel across the Atlantic, it was the use of trends within AIMS which enabled executives to forecast the extent of market downturn. As a result, British Airways launched a successful marketing initiative (the 'Go for it America' campaign) encouraging US citizens to travel when other competing carriers were cutting down on their Atlantic flights.

11.2.3 Current status

Since 1987, AIMS usage amongst British Airways top executives has declined. However, the system is now used widely amongst senior-middle managers (see Figure 11.1). As a result, AIMS has had to be adapted to deal with the wider and more analytical requirements of its current customer base. This has been successfully achieved. However, the change of customer base has moved AIMS from an EIS to a primarily MIS/DSS design focus.

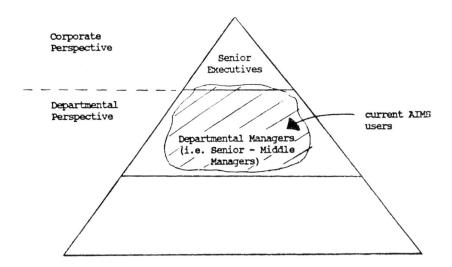

Fig. 11.1 Movement of AIMS usage from executive to senior-middle management levels.

The current generation of AIMS users have also become more technically aware and are increasingly asking for the ability to extract and analyse data residing within AIMS in a more flexible way (e.g. via transfer into spreadsheets). As a result, the AIMS technical platform is now currently under review.

11.2.4 Issues and pitfalls arising from the AIMS initiative

Timing the initiative
Figure 11.2 represents how the fortunes of the AIMS system have changed as a function of state of the business, and executive business knowledge and perception of change.

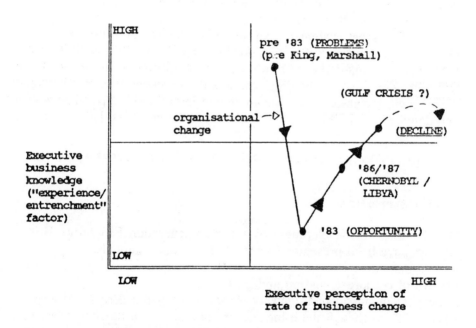

Fig. 11.2 Timing of the AIMS initiative: changing fortunes.

Although the 'normal' EIS developer may not have a crystal ball to hand for prophesying impending organizational change or critical events external to the business, there are a number of general lessons to be drawn from the AIMS initiative:

- The EIS should be seen primarily as an investment which pays off when it positively contributes to competitive advantage in a volatile business environment, through the provision of focused and timely information.
- EIS opportunities are greater when new and influential executives arrive on the scene offering different models for running the business, but at the same time requiring rapid growth in personal knowledge of the business.
- EIS opportunities are less when executives are long established and have an entrenched management style ('We've always done it this way ...' 'It would never work ...').

Gaining effective sponsorship
The manner of AIMS confirms this classic criterion for EIS suc cess. For without Levin's initiative and persuasion, it is unclear how British Airways executives could have been influenced to use AIMS.

Defining the target customers and designing the EIS accordingly
As outlined earlier, movement of AIMS usage down the organization has necessarily changed the system's design requirements to those of an MIS/DSS. The lesson to be drawn here is the necessity of establishing and linking a clear picture of the workstyle and information requirements of a well-defined target EIS customer base to the design of the EIS.

11.3 SECOND-GENERATION EIS: THE MERLIN SYSTEM

11.3.1 Opportunities

Opportunities for development of a second-generation EIS within British Airways have been presented by the following developments:

Launch of corporate mission and goals
A new set of mission and goals were launched within British Airways in April 1989. Although these included restatement of a number of existing company objectives, the launch was accompanied by a serious intention, promoted by the Corporate Strategy Unit, to ensure that corporate performance against goals should be measured and tracked, and directly linked to a well-defined corporate planning process.

New executives on the scene
In the last two years a number of external director appointments have been made to key roles within British Airways, thus bringing in new perspectives for running the business.

Focus on forecasting and tracking performance against agreed key performance measures
Soon after his arrival in 198, one of the external appointments, Liam Strong (now Director of Marketing and Operations) emphasized the importance of having agreed key performance measures and ratios in position for discussing company performance at the executive level. Strong had expressed dissatisfaction at the undue amount of time spent debating the origin and accuracy of figures rather than taking these as read and focusing on decision making and action.

Favourable developments in Information Technology
Advances in IT could now allow the development of a PC-based computer interface which is considerably easier to use than traditional mainframe devices. In particular there was now scope for developing integrated graphical and textual ('windows') interfaces based on the use of touch or mouse-pointing devices. With care, such an interface could reasonably be designed for direct use by top British Airways executives.

11.3.2 Scope

As a result of these opportunities, the MERLIN second-generation EIS is being designed:
- In-house;
- For direct use by British Airways top 40-50 executives;
- To track and forecast performance for agreed corporate level key performance measures;
- To support individual executive 'daily briefing' information needs.

11.3.3 Positioning relative to AIMS

As stressed earlier, MERLIN will complement AIMS (see Figure 11.3).

MERLIN	AIMS
Targeted at top 40-50 executives	Targeted at departmental managers/business analysts
Top level corporate focus	Top level departmental focus within the 'smokestacks'
Strategic focus	Tactical focus
Overview ⇒ Touch/mouse	Analytical ⇒ keyboard
Personalizable	Generalized
Flag issues	Solve flagged issues through more detailed analysis

Fig. 11.3 Comparison of MERLIN and AIMS.

11.3.4 History of promotion and delivery

Initial attempts/pitfalls encountered
Initial attempts (1987 onwards) at promoting a second-generation EIS suffered from the following deficiencies:
- An undue technical focus;
- A lack of information strategy;
- A lack of sustained contact with top executives;
- Little prospect of sponsorship.

Breakthrough
The major opening came in early 1989 when Strong enquired as to what was happening with EIS in British Airways. A presentation was immediately arranged and the outcome was a statement of support from Strong for the EIS initiative.

Sponsorship — the MERLIN champions group
Strong's support for the EIS initiative set the ball rolling. Shortly after the presentation to him, the Director of Information Management stressed the importance of positioning a Group of Champions to drive the MERLIN project from the customer side, and to have the following credentials:

- Directors or direct reports of directors;
- A representative cross-section of the business;
- Are more easily approachable by the MERLIN team.

The Deputy Director of Marketing was appointed Chairman of the Champions Group and presented the MERLIN business proposal to the Executive Policy forming group in October 1989. Subsequently, the Policy Group charged the Champions Group with:

- Quantifying the newly launched corporate goals in terms of key performance measures;
- Trialling the MERLIN system on their behalf.

The Champions Group would also be utilized by the MERLIN project team for prototyping MERLIN and promoting it as the vehicle for executive access to corporate level key performance measures.

Project milestones to date
Milestones to date for the two phases of the MERLIN project are summarized below:

Oct 89: MERLIN proposal presented at executive Policy Group
GREEN light given for Phase 1: Deliver MERLIN prototype
to Champion Group
AMBER light given for Phase 2: Deliver working system to
top executives

May 90:	Phase 1 is delivered to Champions
May to Aug 90:	Champions trial and promote MERLIN
Sep 90:	Phase 2 is formally approved
Mar 91:	Phase 2 target delivery date.

11.3.5 Information and technology design principles

Quantifying corporate goals in terms of key performance measures for inclusion in MERLIN
The procedure adopted for aiding the Champions Group in quantifying corporate goals into key performance measures was as follows (see Figure 11.4). For each goal, the Champions were asked to determine the following:
(1) Key Performance Areas:

What areas the company needs to perform well in, in order to achieve the particular goal.

(2) Key Performance Measures:

Each key performance area would be broken down into sub-areas until it was possible to specify each sub-area in terms of a precise measure of performance.

(3) Overall Measure:

A single key performance measure which best exemplified the extent to which the company was in the long term moving towards the goal.

The MERLIN project team role in this exercise was one of facilitation, and in ensuring that each key performance measure had the following properties agreed by the Champions Group:

● Definition
● Source
● Identity of provider
● Representation (maximizing the use of trend with report backup)
● Target (where appropriate).

These key performance measure properties would then be used in the design of MERLIN's information content.

At the time of writing the above exercise had been completed for three of the seven corporate goals. Director level sign-off of this work has not yet been achieved.

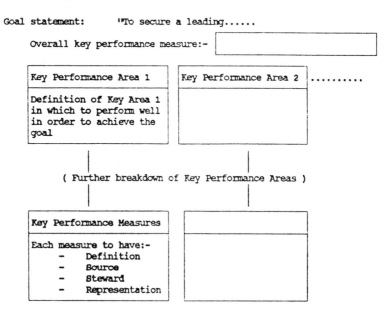

Fig. 11.4 Quantifying British Airways goals into key performance areas and measures.

System design

From the user perspective, MERLIN design is in terms of a newspaper analogy (Figure 11.5). On entry into MERLIN the user is given a set of briefing headlines flagging key business issues. If the executive's attention is grabbed by one of these headlines he/she may then delve into MERLIN in order to track the fuller picture.

Figure 11.6 provides a summary of MERLIN technical design.

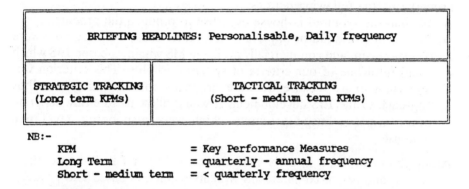

Fig. 11.5   MERLIN design from the user perspective is based on a newspaper analogy.

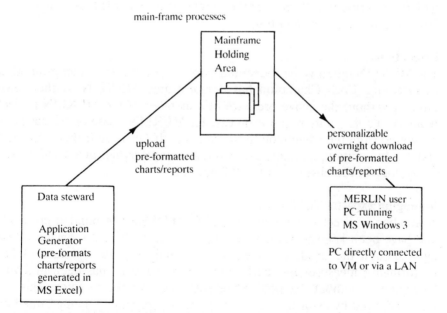

Fig. 11.6   MERLIN technical design.

11.3.6 Summary of issues and pitfalls

EIS issues and pitfalls which have arisen so far from the MERLIN experience (in addition to those discussed in Section 11.2.4) are as follows:

Build or buy?
For both the AIMS and MERLIN developments, our decision has been to build the product in-house. The MERLIN build decision was based primarily on the following reasons:
- We had the required in-house expertise to produce the product.
- At the time of build-or-buy evaluation (early 1989) we were not aware of a successful and commercially available MS windows-based EIS which could fulfil one of our criteria of system flexibility. This criterion was important to us because we were originally contemplating a toolbox approach to the EIS development. It would allow us to easily integrate other windows-based products which were also being developed in-house.

Although our decision in early 1989 was to build our EIS in-house, there are now a number of commercially available windows-based EIS products which would fulfil our criteria. Our early experience with MERLIN has demonstrated the danger of a technical rather than information focus to an EIS project. For this reason I would strongly urge a buy decision for a new EIS development unless there is considerable confidence in the IT function's technical capabilities.

Promotion
The MERLIN initiative has benefited from its Champions' direct promotion to directors. Each Champion has demonstrated MERLIN to their own director without the active presence of a member of the MERLIN project team. As a result, a more powerful case for MERLIN's ease of use has been presented from the Champion to his director ('If I can use it then why can't you?'). In addition, directors feel more at ease in trying their hand at new technology in the absence of the 'IT boffin'!

Managing expectations
A number of directors who have seen MERLIN have responded positively and have been keen to know when they can have MERLIN on their desk even though the product currently shows only a partial picture of key performance measures for the business. The challenge has been in saying 'no, not yet' without dampening the enthusiasm of the director. This has been achieved by assuring the director that the product is being honed on their behalf by his representative on the Champions Group.

Informationo-riented strategy

The MERLIN project has benefited from executive concern to have agreed key performance measures. Without this it is unclear as to what would have been the information focus within MERLIN. The key aspects of our information strategy have been as follows:

- Executive buy-in to key performance measures;
- The need for MERLIN information to have clear added value over existing sources and representations available to the executive;
- The need for effective support for timely provision of information;
- The ability of the system to respond to possible change in key performance information requirements.

11.4 CONCLUSION

One of the major lessons which can be drawn from our experience of EIS evolution in British Airways is that EIS will prove a successful investment through identifying and making the best of opportunities arising in the executive customer base and within the business itself.

These opportunities may arise fortuitously, but in any event it is the ability of the EIS developer to respond speedily and flexibly that will determine his or her ability to succeed in their enterprise.

I hope the experience I have related of the AIMS and MERLIN initiatives will have provided one or two insights into how one may detect and successfully respond to such opportunities.

12 User experience in implementing EIS

D. Stone
British Telecom

The background to this paper is the four EIS implementations that my team and I have implemented within the BT group during the last year and a half. These developments have been completed without the help of external consultancies and are based on the Holos package from Holistic Systems in Ealing.

We were originally asked to investigate EIS in order to attempt to reduce the paper burden that our directors suffered from. The reports that they receive can be measured both terms of inches of thickness as well as the decision window that all reports arrive in and need to react to. This improvement, in some cases, is a saving of between five and ten days, has been the easy part of the job. The difficulty will be saving half the days from this timescale as we move towards 'Online Management', if, that is, the business managers decide to run the business. Whilst there are many common themes between the development and implementation of the BT EI Systems and other EIS implementations, the one lack of commonality seems to be the definition of what constitutes an EIS. My view is that EIS can only be defined by, first, the number of users and, second, certain core, distinct features that the system provides.

12.1 EIS DEFINED

The prime statement is that an EIS delivers information to the top managers of a company. In terms of our system to date that has meant that less than 20 to 25 people have been provided access to any system. In terms of a company that employs 230,000 people, I would expect to provide access to a top team of between 100 and 125 people, but this would be only 0.05% of BT's employees.

The core features that I see as integral to an EIS definition, are those that overcome the two main business problems of data saturation and how to get IT into the boardroom. These are:

1. Ease of use. Without this feature the EIS will not be used. At all times the computer software/operating system must be transparent to the user. The objective of an EIS is to have the learning curve 'peak within minutes' at the outset.

2. Consistency. The EIS must have one standard look and feel throughout the system. This goes from such a high-level design decision as always having the same colour for good, bad or indifferent performance, to the lowest level of always using the same pixel address for headings. An example of the problem that colour coding can bring is: should a competitor's good performance be shown as green for good (it is for them) or red for bad (it is for us)?

3. Exception reporting. This feature enables the EIS to reduce a 200-page report to an understandable and digestible unit. This requires there to be good colour graphics as well as the ability to hold the underlying data so that a deeper investigation of a troublesome area can be undertaken.

4. Homeostatic Reporting. Certain processes/activities within a company may be of such vital importance that constant monitoring is required; should anything go wrong with them, immediate notification or a flash report can be generated and delivered via the EIS.

12.2   SYSTEM ARCHITECTURE

EIS is widely recognized as an essential management tool throughout the business world, and all major companies either have one or are developing an offering. As a result of their proliferation a certain style in the systems architecture has emerged which results from the specific requirements that EIS fulfils.

As has already been mentioned, the problem that faces all EIS developments is the balancing act between too much data, which swamps the executive, and too little which then results in the EIS becoming a useless toy. This common problem is addressed by defining a specific functional architecture that supports all the needs of the users. This architecture falls into three discrete functional elements:

1. A delivery vehicle which consists of proprietary or in-house EIS software, which provides all the expected features.

2. A decision support database, which will support the delivery vehicle with lower level data.

3. A collection vehicle to assemble the required data from the source systems.

This functional architecture, from our point of view, then imposes a structure on the hardware that is needed to support these business requirements. The delivery vehicle needs to be a combination of PC, which will provide the required local power and facilities, and a host machine which also runs the EIS software and assembles the data into a multi-dimensional model ready for delivery. The host machine must also be capable of running the software that will provide the decision support needs of the system. It is also conceivable that the host could undertake the data collection requirements from a number of source systems, but this is probably only applicable to the smaller systems and such a decision would be dependent on a system-sizing exercise.

12.3 INTERNAL PROSPECTIVE

With the prerequisites in mind, I believe that there are a number of ways that the EIS developer can influence the environment for success. These are, in essence, design nuances which range from the right business computing blend of people in terms of business and computing knowledge to delivery timescales.

The perception of EIS developments when they are completed 'in-house' is totally different from the current view of the consultancy-developed EI systems; EIS consultancies hold that EIS developments go hand in hand with the identification and implementation of Critical Success Factors (CSFs). This difference is critical and leads to the creation of a totally different development environment or methodology. This difference is produced by the presence of two underlying factors. First, by virtue of the fact that 'in-house' development terms are members of the company and the initial learning curve that a consultancy has to climb does not exist. Second, an immediate impact is not so vital and so CSFs are not an issue at the outset. This does not detract from the value of the analysis of CSFs, as this work still has to be done; nor does it devalue the work that consultancies can have in the development of CSFs within certain companies. What the 'in-house' perspective does allow is time. This time can then be used to move from a known and comfortable information area that is initially encompassed by the EIS, to a less familiar, but more focused area that involves the analysis of revised critical success factors. This time may also help users to internalize the EIS and get the board to own the eventual result.

In other words why attempt two changes simultaneously and thus have a greater possibility of failure? If the first change is bedded-in properly, then the second will be brought about by internal questioning. This second process will be part of the added value that the EIS brings.

12.4   PROTOTYPING/ITERATION

It is often perceived that computing has failed in the past to deliver to business managers or that the business has not received real value from its investment in IT, and that there has always been a gulf between what is required and what is delivered. This may also be why board room systems are very thin on the ground as the confidence level is missing.

The arrival of four and five GL tools provides a way of getting a closer fit to the needs of the users. The way to activate this opportunity is through developing small prototypes and iterating the prototype with the user. An EIS is not just a system, it is something that is personally tailored for each individual user. User tasks and needs have to be built into the system from the start. This can be done only by iterating the system with each user. Iteration meetings are ideally short in nature and occur at frequent intervals of, for example, two thirty-minute meetings per week during a four-week development cycle. These meetings are ideally held early or late in the day to suit the director and are one of the real costs of an EIS project in terms of his or her time. These meetings do require great user commitment, but they also ensure user 'buy in' as they see their ideas coming to fruition quickly.

The EIS is there to deliver information into the boardroom. The directors are used to delivery on time and expect delivery dates to be met. If a track record of timely delivery is established then the confidence level of the boardroom in the developers is increased.

12.5   BUSINESS SYNERGY

The make-up of the EIS development team must be carefully looked at so that the business needs can be understood. BT's solution was to carefully blend selected computing people, with business people who were recruited on the premise that in developing the EIS there would be an opportunity for them to get all-round experience of the company. These business managers then allow the EIS group to trade on equal terms with our customers. A successful EIS needs this communication of business to business; user to developer. The selection of the computing professionals is just as important as it is they who have the burden of design and developments alongside the naive computing managers.

The issue of sponsorship is also a key concept. An EIS development must have a high-level champion, who is prepared to work with the development team as the system is developed. This active support will not only ensure that the system does reflect the work of the director but it also provides the development team with a certain amount of authority when dealing with, for example, difficult data suppliers.

12.6 TOP-DOWN ANALYSIS

An EIS is built to answer the needs of top managers of any company. To achieve this the work of each director must be examined alongside an investigation of the strategy of the company. The relevant source data can then be collected and presented within an EIS framework. This data collection area is probably the hardest and least rewarding work element within an EIS development. Nevertheless, an EIS without data cannot exist and so the collection of data is one of the crucial tasks of the job.

Again there is conflict with the traditional systems department within this area. An argument that is often used is that EI Systems cannot be developed until the bottom, or source, level of data has been established as quality data. In other words a corporate data dictionary produced and the bottom-up analysis completed. The question that is always posed is how can an EIS be built on data that is inconsistent, inaccurate, misdefined or just blatantly wrong?

The answer to this is relatively simple. The company has managed to continue in this environment and has developed manual reports that hold and deliver this data. The EIS will not improve the situation, but it will provide the best spotlight on the problem and hence gain top-level support to improve the situation. The problem is not one of bad data, but one of having bad data and of making a decision based on it without knowing the data is bad. If cornerstones of good data can be found and the EIS can mark the dubious data, e.g. as gold, silver or bronze relating to the quality, then a reasonable picture of the company's performance can be produced.

12.7 SPEED OF RESPONSE

This paragraph does not relate to the usual sub-five-seconds response time for on-line systems, although it is worth mentioning that the EIS must be beneath this threshold. This refers to the nature of the people that the EIS is aimed at. In general, they have managed to get to a very senior position, by delivering to the usually very short timescales. The EIS development team has to echo this.

There are many ways that a development team can influence the environment to help delivery. four and five GL tools have already been discussed and these tools will allow an extremely speedy response to the customers' needs. As well as this the bureaucracy within a project can be cut to the bone. A statement of requirements is not needed, an outline system description can be done without and, finally, a detailed system specification is also not required. The various stages of a project have been drummed into computing staff as have the time lengths associated with each stage. In an EIS environment these are a positive hindrance. I also firmly believe that this statement is valid outside the EIS arena as well as within it.

The way to document the project is purely through a project diary. This electronic or manual system documents all that happens within the project. In the dynamic EIS environment the project diary is the only way that documentation can keep pace with a rapidly evolving system as each prototype is iterated. Some customers may find this level of documentation too bureaucratic, but they can be won round once they realize the significance of the diary. Once this has been established, a 'design trail' becomes apparent, and this can be used by a specialist technical writer to produce the appropriate documentation.

Another way to shorten timescales is to implement the quality maxim 'One bite at a time' or, as we prefer it, 'The Lego approach'. By separating any project into its smallest units timescales can be equally shortened. The customer does not care what programming is delivered, all that is wanted is company data in an understandable format. If a block at a time is delivered, then any new block must be added transparently to the already existing EIS. They will need to know what new features or reports have been added, but it must not change the overall EIS environment design as any change may well lose the user.

12.8   LOOKING FORWARD

At this moment EIS in BT seems to have been a success, but the processes that have been used to bring this to fruition are applicable to a much wider field than EIS. The days of directors supporting computing developments through 'acts of faith' are long gone. If a computing development is worth investment then let it show a bottom-line improvement.

If this is to be the view of the 1990s then Rapid Development Methodologies (RDM) and prototyping are the only way that the computing industry can go. The 'act of faith' needed for a £100K prototype is much less than the one needed for a £10 million development, but if the prototype demonstrates the likely benefits that will accrue from the £10 million project then it can go ahead. If it does not show these benefits then the project can be cancelled with marginal loss.

This entrepreneurial attitude must be recognized within computing. IT can deliver real benefits and RDM may well prove to be the main channel that will allow IT to do this during the 1990s.

The basic message from the coalface is that EIS is needed by large companies and can be successfully delivered in-house. This success depends on:

a. A successful business/computing relationship.

b. The use of Rapid Development Methodologies.

c. The act of support of one or more sponsors.

13 Determining information systems priorities with decision conferencing

N. Tout
ICL Executive Education

13.1 INTRODUCTION

There is growing evidence of senior management concern by ensuring that information technology (IT) investments provide value for money and that its usage is directly related to an organization's strategic direction. In the UK this concern is by no means restricted to the private sector. Privatization moves and government legislation in local authorities has meant that many public bodies are as equally concerned with the most effective utilization of scarce resources.

In this paper we explore how a growing number of organizations are using an intensive style of workshop, known as Decision Conferencing, to help senior management develop a shared understanding of their IT investment priorities.

13.2 BACKGROUND

One source of management concerns regarding IT is the annual survey undertaken by the consultants Price Waterhouse (1990). This shows that 'integrating IT with corporate strategy' is the top issue, having overtaken 'meeting project deadlines' which was the top issue for much of the 1980s. The same report, when discussing the problem of putting a value on corporate information, quotes Dr David Silk of Henley Management College:

'The trouble with information is that it is not readily quantifiable. Unlike the other types of assets a manager deals with, its value is both intangible and subjective.'

So, as we see, the level of investment in information systems and services growing from the average of 3% of turnover in the 1970s to a figure of over 5% for many organizations as we enter the turbulent 1990s, the use of cost criteria for evaluating IT is becoming increasingly obsolete. What is needed are new approaches that focus on the value that management perceive can be derived from information systems.

This shift in the importance attached to the different benefits associated with IT investment can be found in a variety of sources. One such survey (Tomlin 1990) is summarized in Figures 13.1 and 13.2. This shows clearly that the sharpest increases are among the benefits concerned with broad business effectiveness. Improving customer service, now the number one priority, has risen in importance by about 30% over the last five years. Other benefits which are externally focused, such as competitive position, product quality and new business opportunities, all show substantial increases in importance.

On the other hand, benefit categories with a cost saving or efficient focus, show smaller percentage rises as well as falling in their relative positions. The survey notes that though these goals may no longer be prime benefits sought from IT investment, many examples from all industry sectors demonstrated how significant these savings have been and the valuable role they will continue to play.

Such concerns are by no means restricted to the private sector. In UK local government, for example, a recent article (Hill 1990) clearly identified the shift in benefits away from cost savings to the softer competitive benefits. The same article also identifies the importance of management judgement in assessing these competitive benefits and that traditional cost-benefit analysis alone is not sufficient for justifying IT investments.

Given this background the question then arises as to how senior management can be assisted in developing a shared understanding of their IT priorities. For the last seven years ICL, through a long-term collaboration with the Decision Analysis Unit at the LSE, has been pioneering the use of Decision Conferencing as a highly effective way of assisting management groups to review their IT investment priorities. Before we look in more detail at a case study, a few words about the general Decision Conferencing process are appropriate.

13.3 WHAT IS IT?

A recent definition of Decision Conferencing is:

A group of people meeting to resolve some issues of concern to their organization, helped by a facilitator and using computer modelling of human judgement, with the goal of achieving a shared understanding of the issues, a sense of common purpose and a commitment to action.

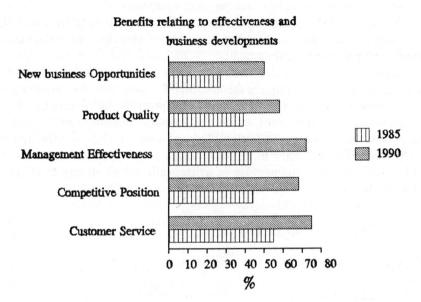

Fig. 13.1 Shifting focus of IT benefits.

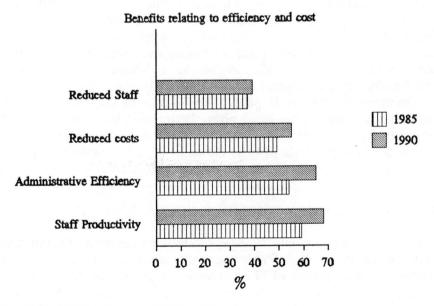

Fig. 13.2 Shifting focus of IT benefits.

A unique feature of this approach is the creation, on the spot, of a computer-based model which incorporates the different perspectives of the participants in the group. As will be seen later from the case studies the models used in information systems prioritization typically focus on the evaluation of alternative resource allocation strategies against multiple benefit criteria of the group's choice.

Events usually take place over a two day period aided by two people from outside the organization, a facilitator and analyst, who are experienced in working with groups. The facilitator helps participants to structure their discussions, identify the issues, model the problem and interpret the results. The analyst uses a portable computer to implement in real-time the models developed by the facilitator in response to the group's input and acts as the conference's recorder to provide a written audit trail of the conference proceedings.

13.4 FACILITIES AND EQUIPMENT

The events can be staged almost anywhere but is typically one of the following:
- An 'off-site' location such as a hotel or conference centre.
- The facilitator's location.
- The client's premises.

Of these the last is least preferred because of the likelihood of distractions by phone calls, visitors and side meetings, all of which have a highly disruptive effect on group working. Experience has also shown that distinct advantages arise from getting the team away overnight so that they have the opportunity to reflect informally on the day's work, to mix informally and thereby engender a sense of team spirit.

Particular attention is paid to the layout of the room with the participants being seated in an open 'U' in front of a set of portable whiteboards (see Figure 13.3.) One of the boards is used for projection from the portable computer via an LCD flat panel on a high-powered overhead projector, so that the group can use the model interactively.

13.5 RELATIONSHIP WITH OTHER EDUCATIONAL EVENTS

Many of the Decision Conferencing events we have run during the last three years for UK clients, as well as for our own management teams, have been devoted to prioritization of IT investment. Often this has been part of a broader executive education programme to equip management teams with an understanding of the growing strategic importance of IT. Such programmes, which are invariably tailored for a particular client, often start with a two-day awareness of IT to ensure management teams appreciate the strategic importance of IT and the role they have in ensuring business benefits are obtained. Typically there would then follow a workshop style event to gain familiarity with a variety of tools and techniques that are of value in integrating IT with the vision and long-term planning for a client organization.

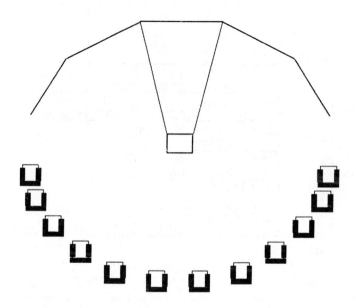

Fig. 13.3 Conference room layout.

The underlying philosophy behind our approach has been to facilitate the application of a number of frameworks that enable management teams in general, and IT steering groups in particular, to relate their organization's use of IT to their business objectives. The last stage of such programmes utilizes the highly participatory Decision Conferencing style of working. Such a participatory approach contrasts strongly with the more prescriptive approaches, often advocated by traditional consultants who are receiving increasing criticism for being ineffective (Carter and Bresnick 1989).

13.6 CASE STUDY

The case study comes from an event run for a major UK service organization. The board of this group had requested recommendations from senior line management as to where IT investment should be put if more resources were made available. During the course of the Decision Conference that was run in response to this requirement the group developed a model shown in Figure 13.4.

			LEVEL		
VARIABLE	1	2	3	4	5
1 A	Status Quo	1 + More of Same	2 + New Areas	2 + Diff't Areas	3 + 4
2 B	Status Quo	Expand	2 + Add'l Facilities	2 + Add'l Equipment	4 + Add'l Facilities
3 C	Status Quo	1 + Other Customers	New System	2 + 3	
4 D	Status Quo	PC Solution	Mini Solution	M/F Solution	
5 E	Status Quo	Extend to New Areas			
6 F	Status Quo	Faster SQ	2 + Link Dep'ts	3 + Ext Links	

Fig. 13.4.

This model shows that the group identified six areas where additional IT investment would generate benefits for their company. For each application area the group generated a range of qualitatively different strategies that would use more resources than their current plans. For example, looking at the sixth area, which was concerned with office systems, the group identified three alternative strategies. First they could speed up their current plans, given more investment they would build on this by starting to link key departments. Finally, the most expensive option they were prepared to consider was to add external electronic mail to remote locations. We find that groups tend to find the exercise of sharing a clear definition of alternatives valuable in its own right as a means of facilitating communication.

The next stage of the process is to define the key cost and benefit criteria that the group wish to use in their evaluations. In this example the cost criteria were readily agreed as being the total revenue costs of the option and the capital costs over the next three years. The agreement on the benefit criteria to be used can be more time consuming and often depends on how clearly the group agrees on the key business objectives for its organization.

In this example the group was readily able to articulate six key objectives and so a composite benefit criterion was agreed for subsequent evaluations. This was defined as the extent to which the investment options supported the achievement of these objectives.

The role of the facilitator at this stage is to aid the group in evaluating the alternatives for each investment against the agreed cost and benefit criteria.

Taking the last of the six areas from our example, Figure 13.5 gives the results of these evaluations. This shows the cumulative revenue and capital costs of the options under the heading of costs. So the option of speeding up the current plan was, for example, estimated as costing £16K revenue and £80K capital. Note also that the approach allows us to give different 'weights' to the two cost criteria as indicated by the bottom row in the figure. This shows that the group judged revenue to be more important than capital by a ratio of 50 to 30. When the model works out, for the group, the overall cost of any option these weights are used to factor the associated costs to give a weighted total that is also shown in Figure 13.5.

Benefits are 'scored' on a relative scale so that 100 represents the option that is most preferred in supporting the six corporate objective, and 0 the least preferred. The other options are then positioned between these two extremes depending on the group's collective judgement. Of course these assessments are by no means simple for the group and much valuable debate takes place as the group explores the differing reasons for the relative positioning of the options.

```
VARIABLE 6: F
                       COST
                       Rev   Cap  TOTAL    Ben
  1 Status Quo          0     0     .0      0
  2 Faster SQ          16    80   32.0     60
  3 2 + Link Dep'ts   106   125   90.5     70
  4 3 + Ext  Links    162   185  136.5    100

    CRITERION WTS                           30
    ACROSS CRITERIA WTS   50    30         100
```

Fig. 13.5.

Having evaluated the costs and benefits for each investment area the next stage of the process is to get the group to judge the relative importance of the benefit differences across the six areas. Once elicited these 'weights' are used to factor the benefit scores so that, for every investment portfolio that takes one option in each area, there is an overall cost and a benefit for that portfolio. The modelling software is then able to generate a cost-benefit plot as shown in Figure 13.6.

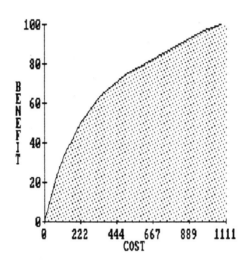

Fig. 13.6.

All 3,200 possible investment portfolios, that take one option from each of the six investment areas, are either in the shaded area or on the curve. Those on the curve represent the most beneficial set of strategies to adopt for a given level of resource usage. Any portfolios that are in the shaded area can be bettered. To illustrate this, let us suppose the group felt intuitively that the 'best' combination of strategies was as shown in Figure 13.7.

The plot of the cost/benefit curve in Figure 13.8 shows that this particular investment package lies well within the shaded area at the point **P**. Two points are of particular interest, first the point **B** which represents a package of comparable cost that gives significantly more benefit. Second, point **C** represents a cheaper combination that gives comparable Benefit to the proposed package. The model also generates for the group details of the combination of strategies that make up packages **B** and **C** as shown in Figure 13.9.

```
                              PROPOSED PACKAGE
              VARIABLE       COST   WTS   BEN LEVEL
        1 A                  70.0   160   120 1 + More of Same     (2 OF 5)
        2 B                    .0   160     0 Status Quo           (1 OF 5)
        3 C                 341.5   267   160 New System           (3 OF 4)
        4 D                  97.8   213   181 M/F Solution         (4 OF 4)
        5 E                    .0   120     0 Status Quo           (1 OF 2)
        6 F                  32.0    80    48 Faster SQ            (2 OF 4)
                            541.3         509
```

Fig. 13.7.

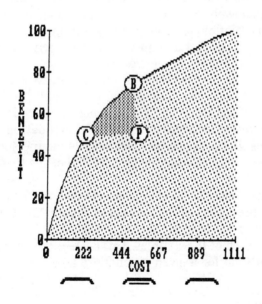

Fig. 13.8.

VARIABLE	1	2	LEVEL 3	4	5
1 A		CP		B	
2 B	CP		B		
3 C	C	B	P		
4 D			CB	P	
5 E	P	CB			
6 F		CPB			

Fig. 13.9.

The cells in this matrix with a **P** in them represent the proposed package, whilst those with a **B** and **C** represent the 'better' and 'cheaper' combinations respectively. So given the group's judgements the model is suggesting that the 'better' package would mean increasing investment in area 1 from level 2 to level 4 and up to level 3 in area 2 and so on noting that the suggested level 2 in area 6 was the right one.

It is often the case that members of the group have different views on some of the benefit scores or, more often, the weights used in the model. One of the values of the Decision Conferencing approach is that the model can be used to test the robustness of accommodating the different perspectives of the group. So, rather than have an interpersonal debate, the focus becomes one of seeing what the model is indicating to the group about their priorities.

Another output that the model generates that was of particular value for this group is the 'order of buy' shown in Figure 13.10. This shows the options that would be bought into as investment is raised above the minimum level in each of the six areas. This enables the group to determine the preferred portfolio for a given expenditure level.

13.7 CONCLUSIONS

The highly participative approach of using Decision Conferencing to assist management teams in determining their Information Systems investment priorities enables opportunities to be evaluated against the softer benefits associated with the use of IT in support of corporate objectives. Tradeoffs can be explored using the model and thereby avoid interpersonal conflicts.

The presence and role of the facilitator as a neutral arbiter provides process rather than content support that enables groups to focus on their work and avoid sterile debates. Many groups have found that the approach helps break through stalemates to achieve shared understanding amongst participants.

#	VARIABLE	ORDER OF BEST PACKAGES LEVEL	COST	CUM COST	CUM % BENEFIT
0	1 A	1 Status Quo	.0	.0	0
0	2 B	1 Status Quo	.0	.0	0
0	3 C	1 Status Quo	.0	.0	0
0	4 D	1 Status Quo	.0	.0	0
0	5 E	1 Status Quo	.0	.0	0
0	6 F	1 Status Quo	.0	.0	0
1	4 D	3 Mini Solution	72.0	72.0	213
2	5 E	2 Extend to New Areas	51.0	123.0	333
3	1 A	2 1 + More of Same	70.0	193.0	453
4	6 F	2 Faster SQ	32.0	225.0	501
5	3 C	2 1 + Other Customers	92.1	317.1	608
6	1 A	4 2 + Diff't Areas	31.0	348.1	640
7	2 B	3 2 + Add'l Facilities	152.5	500.6	744
8	2 B	5 4 + Add'l Facilities	117.0	617.6	800
9	3 C	4 2 + 3	341.5	959.1	960
10	1 A	5 3 + 4	21.5	980.6	968
11	6 F	4 3 + Ext Links	104.5	1085.1	1000

Fig. 13.10.

REFERENCES

Carter, W.B. and Bresnick, T.A. (1989) Strategic planning conferences *Business Horizons*, September/October 1989.

Hill, P. (1990) *Measuring the Intangible Local Government Chronicle*, 21 September 1990.

Price Waterhouse (1990) *Information Technology Review 1989/90*, Price Waterhouse.

Tomlin, R. (1990) *Clues to Success − A Corporate Culture for Information Technology* Ahdahl Executive Institute, February.

14 The Southern Isle Financial Services Company; amending the Gorry And Scott Morton framework

C. Murphy
University College, Cork

14.1 INTRODUCTION

DSS is a discipline which has evolved from the less than successful experiences with Management Information Systems and Operations Research. It represents an attempt by computer professionals and management scientists to make an important contribution to the improvement of the managerial function within organizations.

The DSS literature has advocated supporting managers rather than replacing them. As Mintzburg put it:

'What appeals to me about the orientation of the DSS literature, in general, is its sympathy with the needs of the manager and its sensitivity to the findings of descriptive research. It is refreshing to see these computer systems recognized as "support" and to encounter a part of the management science literature that puts down neither the manager nor his intuition. This provides a healthy basis on which to develop and introduce these systems into organizational decision making. ... Maybe the DSS people with their managerial orientation, can rediscover what operations research seems to have lost'[Min82].

14.2 THE FRAMEWORK OF GORRY AND SCOTT MORTON

Many of the concepts and definitions of DSS are based on the pioneering work of Anthony Gorry and Michael Scott Morton. In their seminal article 'A framework for management information systems', Gorry and Scott Morton developed a framework that has become the foundation stone for much of the research work in DSS. In developing their framework they made use of the work of Anthony on the three levels of managerial activity and Simon's work on programmed and non-programmed decisions [Ant65], [Sim47], [Sim67].

They analysed decisions in terms of Anthony's categorization of managerial activity and Simon's classification of programmed and non-programmed decisions. They defined structured decision systems as those used to support fully structured problems, i.e. those problems where it is possible to specify algorithms or decision rules that allow the problem to be found, alternative solutions to be designed and the best solution to be selected. They compared these with decision support systems which are designed to support unstructured or semi-structured problems, i.e. those problems where little or nothing is known about the problem situation [GM71].

They represented their framework as shown in Table 14.1.

Table 14.1 Gorry and Scott Morton's framework for information systems.

	Operational Control	Management Control	Strategic Control
Structured	Accounts Receivable	Budget Analysis Engineered Costs	Tanker Fleet Mix
	Order Entry	Short Term Forecasting	Warehouse and Factory Location
	Inventory Control		
Semi-Structured	Production Scheduling	Variance Analysis – Overall Budget	Mergers and Acquisitions
	Cash Management	Budget Preparation	New Product Planning
Unstructured	PERT COST Systems	Sales and Production	R and D Planning

They suggested that a framework such as the one they were proposing was essential. 'A framework which allows an organization to gain perspective on the field of information systems can be a powerful means of providing focus and improving the effectiveness of the system efforts.' Their framework was seized upon by researchers of DSS as a key to defining what DSS was about. From the 1970s right through to the 1990s, DSS researchers have used their framework.

In 1980 Sprague [Spr80] suggested that decision support systems should provide support for decision making, but with the emphasis on semi-structured and unstructured decisions that upper-level managers typically face.

Ginzberg and Stohr in 1982 stated that, 'DSS is a computer-based information system used to support decision-making activities in situations where it is not possible or desirable to have an automated system perform the entire decision process'[GS82].

Hogue suggested that DSS 'supports but does not replace managerial decision making' and that it is directed towards semi-structured and/or unstructured decision or related decisions [Hog82].

Srinivasan and Kim in 1986 stated that, 'However, as research and practice in DSS have evolved, it is now recognized to be a system that supports all the relevant aspects of a decision process or processes. The extent of support could range from being purely descriptive in the case of unstructured aspects to being prescriptive in the case of structured aspects'[SK86].

We can see from the above that the Gorry and Scott Morton frame-work has and continues to be the fundamental concept underlying the definitions of DSS. As Kirs et al. described it, 'the Gorry and Scott Morton framework is perhaps the best known, most durable and most frequently cited in the IS field' [K*89].

However, there has been some criticism of their work. Moore and Chang argued:

'DSS scholars ... have attempted to apply this structured/programmed distinction as a criterion for classifying potential DSS problem areas — the conventional wisdom being that a DSS is appropriate for semi-structured decision problems. This in turn has stimulated an attempt by both scholars and practitioners to classify all decision-making situations by a sort of structured/unstructured criterion, an activity we consider to be largely fruitless and a major source of confusion in the DSS literature. This confusion is also evident in Simon's notation of programmed versus non-programmed decisions. As we see it, a problem can only be considered more or less structured with regard to a particular decision maker, or group of similar decision makers and at a particular point in time. In our experience there is simply no structure that can be identified with any decision-making problem independent of the decision maker. ... Thus we believe it is both incorrect and misleading for DSS designers to speak of structured or programmed problems in the general case when approaching a DSS design situation' [MC83].

This view was endorsed by Keen. He stated that '... Gorry-Scott Morton "model" of structured, semi-structured and unstructured tasks which played a key role in launching the decision support systems movement is simply wrong' [Kee87].

14.3 RESEARCH AIMED AT DEVELOPING A FRAMEWORK

The objective of the research reported in this chapter was to develop a framework which, while building on the work of Gorry and Scott Morton, would take account of the specific situation within an organization and would allow the DSS personnel to evaluate how successful they have been within their own organization.

In developing a framework which is valid for each specific organization it is necessary to have a view of the types of decision support systems that are used in each organization. Much of the reported empirical DSS research has focused on the development of a once-off system rather than on a number of systems over a period of time in one organization. Reporting on one system does not give an insight into how DSS is actually being used within an organization and does not help in developing a framework for DSS. Nor is it possible if one accepts Moore and Chang's criticisms to develop a framework based on such decision support systems as have been reported in the literature since each of those comes from a different organization.

To overcome this problem the approach taken in this study was to conduct an action research project in 'The Southern Isle Financial Services Company'. The project involved the development of four decision support systems over a three-year period. This work was carried out by the researcher with the assistance of a team of research assistants. In essence the researcher became the DSS person within the organization. The decision support systems and the issues associated with their development are summarized below.

14.4 THE FIELD RESEARCH

The field research was undertaken within 'The Southern Isle Financial Services Company'. This is part of a large financial services group, 'The Emerald Isle Financial Services Company'. The group is organized on a geographical basis, with Ireland divided into five areas which are in turn split into a number of regions. Each region has a number of branches, typically between 20 and 30. While the majority of policies are formulated at group headquarters in Dublin, considerable autonomy is given to the areas in running their business. Each area would be comparable to the position of a company which forms part of a group. The Southern Isle Financial Services Company is one of the areas.

The Southern Isle company is headed by a general manager to whom four assistant managers report directly. These, in turn, have a large number of managers reporting to them.

The work with the Southern Isle company commenced when the management approached the researcher suggesting that a number of problems that they faced could be addressed more thoroughly if they had better quality information which, they thought, could be provided by computer-based systems to support them.

14.4.1 DSS 1

Following initial discussions it was agreed that the researcher should develop a system (known as 'The Company Database System') which would expand the analysis capability of the company's executives and support staff in monitoring the company's branches. Specifically, the system would help managers in assessing both the shortterm and longterm performances of the regions and the area.

In the discussions with senior management a number of new performance measures were identified which were more market-oriented than their existing measures.

From the nature of the information requirements, as expressed at the various management levels, the researcher, with the help of some research assistants, developed a view of the analysis and reporting capability. The main aspects were short- and long-term analyses of performance by overall area, each region and individual branch.

A feature of the system was that it allowed peer group assessment. This involved grouping a number of branches who, in the opinion of the managers, were similar and for whom they would expect similar growth patterns and performance. They reckoned that this would make it easier for them to make comparisons than if they were looking at all branches in a region simultaneously.

The system was to be accessible on micro-computers in each of the regional offices as well as the head office. The management were given the flexibility to decide which reports they would look at. The results and key features of the system could be presented in either tabular or graphical format. The user, i.e. a manager or a member of the support staff, could specify which format they preferred.

Four years after it was implemented, senior managers are still using the system with some modifications.

14.4.2 DSS 2

The second system developed was technically similar to the first in that it was a flexible analysis and reporting system that allowed management to specify their information requirements and the format in which the information was to be presented. This illustrates that there is no automatic progression from what was basically a reporting system to some more technically challenging system. The system was developed for the area credit department. This department is run by the area credit controller who has responsibility for the issuing of major loans through all of the 90 branches and monitors the lending performance of branch managers. At the time of the development of the system the operations of the credit department were regarded as being of the utmost importance because the general economic situation in Ireland and in particular the poor state of the agricultural sector had resulted in all financial institutions raising their bad-debts provision and placing much greater emphasis on the control and management of their loan portfolios.

The credit controller, when asked for the type of system he wished to have, replied 'I want the type of system that was developed for the company database with the requirements that I have specified.' The requirements which the credit controller specified were:

1. To provide a system with the capacity to perform exception reporting;
2. To provide a system with the capacity to perform trend analysis;
3. To include new information which would allow a profile of a branch to be assessed over the past thirteen months;
4. To provide a graphic capability; and
5. A flexible reporting system.

Much of the data to be inputted originated from computer-generated reports. This is consistent with the findings of Quillard et al. who found that more than half the information keyed in by end-users originated from computer-generated reports [Q*83].

These requirements were relatively clear and unambiguous and the development strategy followed was much the same as for the initial system.

The credit controller took very much of a hands-off approach to the development of the system. This was based on his high level of trust in the development group. This trust was based on his perception of the earlier system that had been produced. When the researcher would point out to him that the system for his department was different because of a different language being used and different information being used, he would respond 'All I want is a system like the company database system.'

The credit control system was implemented very successfully and has been used ever since.

14.4.3 DSS 3

The first two systems which were developed were ones that could be almost totally specified after initial investigation. The next two systems came from processes which were quite different.

The third system was developed for one of the regional managers. This system was different from the two previous ones in that it emerged out of a process where the researcher interacted with the regional manager and his staff to identify problems which needed to be addressed, and established how these might be tackled. The manager's perceived requirement was the need for him to be capable of assessing the performance of the branches under his control. He required that this assessment should be a weighted view of a number of factors. However, in the past they found it very difficult to specify what parameters should be used to get an equitable measurement system. The researcher was asked to develop a number of measurement systems which were then tested and evaluated by the manager and his staff. The overall system was developed using a prototype approach. Its main features were:

A ranked performance analysis, devised to determine how a branch was performing relative to every other branch in the same region. All branches were ranked according to their percentage growth figures under certain headings and an overall performance score was also calculated. This score was to be calculated by assigning a weighting to each of the above performance measures.

The problem addressed was a serious issue which had confronted management for some time and had caused difficulty. In particular it allowed senior management to devise an overall rating system for assessing the overall performance of branches. A major benefit of the system was that management could change, in the light of changing economic circumstances, the parameters to be used in calculating the overall rating. The system continues to be used to rank and analyse the performance of branches.

14.4.4 DSS 4

The fourth system to be developed was of a fundamentally different type to those previously outlined. This system evolved out of a process in which senior management in the area were concerned with the type and quality of information that they would need to implement a market segmentation programme. Under this programme, the various product and services which Southern Isle were offering were to be differentiated largely on an age basis, with some products also related to the type of occupation that people had. Management were particularly concerned with planning for this programme and assessing the performance of the branches for each product. The researcher and postgraduate assistant spent considerable time with management attempting to determine an appropriate way to address the issue. The process followed was very much an exploratory one with both groups required to come to grips with a difficult problem for which there was no obvious solution or relevant internal information. As part of this process the researcher and student brought forward a number of suggestions and presented them to management.

One of the suggestions which emerged from the process was that use would be made of external information such as that available from census data. It was thought that this information, coupled with managers' experience, would enable them to develop a management system that would help them in the planning, delivery and monitoring of new products.

It was agreed to develop a computer-based system which would provide demographic information on target markets in order to support planning and control decisions by managers at branch, region, company and group level. The system was to be designed so as to allow managers maximum scope in retrieving strategic marketing information.

The resulting system, MAPS (Market Analysis and Planning System), is a computer-based system developed to support strategic market analysis and planning. The system uses computer mapping facilities to enable managers to define and analyse specific target markets using demographic data derived from the census of population. MAPS allows the managers to call up maps of the various counties or market areas to outline branch catchment areas using the directional keys on the keyboard. The manager can then access a range of demographic data and graphs for the area outlined. MAPS is particularly useful in the following areas:

1. Comparing the total population of a defined area with the company's customer numbers to assess its overall penetration of the market in the area;

2. Identifying new target markets; and

3. Assisting with new product development, since an essential part of any new product evaluation is the structure of the market in terms of size and demographic structure.

14.5 A FRAMEWORK FOR THE PROBLEMS ADDRESSED

The four systems which were developed are broadly similar in technical terms, yet they varied in terms of their contribution to the company. The existing frameworks/definitions for DSS, based on the Gorry and Scott Morton framework, do not help to categorize these four systems. This is because those frameworks categorize decision support systems in terms of their technical components or because they attempt to categorize decisions in the generic terms of structured/unstructured decisions which fail to take account of specific organizational factors. All of the problems which were addressed were ones that were viewed as important by senior management. All systems were used by the same levels of management and in terms of Simon's classification could be categorized as semi-structured.

Two aspects of the problem were identified which appeared to influence the usefulness of the contribution made by the systems to the management of the company. These were the novelty of the problem and its specificity. Novelty in this instance refers to the prior experience which the management in the company had with this type of problem. Thus the first system, the area database system, was used to address a problem with which managers had considerable experience. In contrast, the MAPS system was used to address issues which were new for the managers and hence they had no specific prior experience, although of course they had their overall business experience and acumen to bring to bear on the problem.

The second factor, the specificity of the problem, is one which is partially related to the first in that if management have had no prior experience of dealing with a problem then they are less likely to be capable of specifying the problem as well as if they have had some experience. In the case of the Southern Isle Financial Services Company the management were able to specify fairly completely the parameters of the problems which the area database system and the credit analysis system were designed to address. The branch performance and MAPS systems were used to address problems which management could only partially specify. This was because of the nature of the problems and/or their novelty. A major benefit for management, from their interaction with the DSS team on these two problems, was a greater understanding of the issues, suggesting that DSS personnel can help the learning process for managers.

These two parameters require the type of framework which is shown in Table 14.2.

Table 14.2.

Specificity of Problem	Frequency of Problem		
	Frequently	Infrequently	Novel
Completely Specifiable	Company Database I	Credit Analysis System II	
Partially Specifiable		Branch Performance Measurement System III	M.A.P.S. IV
Very Difficult To Specify			

This framework is different to those given in DSS studies. It is a framework which allows for an organization's specific experience of dealing with these types of problems. In the case of The Southern Isle Financial Services Company the problems addressed by the management and the DSS researcher were ones which could at least be partially specified. However, the involvement of the researcher in addressing a novel problem was encouraging. When management were asked why they had used the researcher for this purpose, they pointed to the strong relationship that had been developed with the DSS researcher and the ease with which they communicated with him.

It was pointed out above that in developing systems there was no guarantee of automatic progression from simple to more technically challenging systems. However, an analysis of Table 14.2 shows that, in terms of the complexity of the problem addressed, there was a significant progression. This reflected the continuous build-up of trust and respect between the researcher and the managers. It also suggests, tentatively at least, that this framework could be used to assess the progress made by DSS staff in organizations.

14.6 FRAMEWORK FOR OTHER COMPANIES

The framework developed for Southern Isle had to be regarded a tentative until it was confirmed or rejected in a wider sample of companies. This evaluation was carried out in ten other companies. In each of the companies, three senior managers were interviewed. The managers were those who participate in the major decisions of their organizations and hence were in a position to assess the extent to which their DSS staff helped in the decision-making processes of their organizations.

Six questions were put to the managers concerning the use made of DSS staff in addressing certain type of problems. The questions and the average response for each company are shown in Table 14.3.

Table 14.3 Use of DSS staff in different problem situations.

Questions	Company									
	A	B	C	D	E	F	G	H	I	J
Faced with a problem we could completely specify we used DSS people	2	2	2	2	2	2	3	4	2	2
Faced with a problem we could partially specify we used DSS people	2	2	3	2	3	2	2	3	2	2
Faced with a problem we could not specify we used DSS people	3	1	4	1	5	2	2	3	3	2
Faced with a significant problem which recurred frequently we sought the assistance of DSS people	3	3	3	3	3	3	2	4	2	2
Faced with a significant problem which recurred infrequently we sought the assistance of DSS people	2	2	3	2	3	2	2	3	2	2
Faced with a problem which was novel we sought the assistance of DSS people	2	1	4	2	4	2	3	3	2	

Key To Table: 1 = always   2 = frequently   3 = sometimes
4 = infrequently   5 = never

The table is divided into two parts. The first three questions were aimed at determining the level of DSS support for varying complexity of problems, and the last three questions were designed to identify the extent to which DSS staff were used to address overall problems which had different degrees of frequency.

An analysis of the first three questions shows that managers in two of the companies (B, D) are very frequent users of the DSS staff. In five of the companies (A, F, G, I and J) the DSS staff are used frequently. In three of the companies (C, E and H) management are reluctant to use their DSS staff.

An analysis of the responses to the questions in the second part of Table 14.4 shows that they are very similar to the pattern of responses for the questions in the first part of the table relating to problem complexity. Managers in seven of the companies (A, B, D, F, G, I and J) are likely to make significant use of DSS staff. In the case of managers in companies B, D and F they are more likely to use them if the problem is more novel than if it is a more regularly occurring problem. This is a strong indication that in these companies DSS staff are regarded as an integral part of the management team.

Table 14.4.

Specificity of Problem	Frequency of Problem		
	Frequently	Infrequently	Novel
Completely Specifiable	C,E, H	All Companies	A, B, D, F G, I, J
Partially Specifiable	All Companies	A, F G, I, J	A, B, D, F G, I, J
Very Difficult To Specify	B, D, G I, J	A, B, D, F G, I, J	B, D

The managers in three of the companies (C, E and H) were less likely to use their DSS staff and in particular used them only infrequently or sometimes for significant problems which were novel.

The responses to these questions allowed the ten companies to be categorized using the framework developed for The Southern Isle Financial Services Company. The results are shown in Table 14.4. This shows that two of the companies (B and D) make use of their DSS staff to address problems that are very difficult to specify and which are novel. Five of the companies (A, F, G, I and J) use their DSS staff to help them to address very difficult problems and which occur infrequently or partially specifiable problems which are novel. In three of the companies (C, E and H) the DSS staff, if used at all, are used to address very well-defined and frequently occurring problems.

14.7 CONCLUSION

These results suggest that the framework which was developed is a useful vehicle for categorizing the role played by DSS staff within organizations. Unlike the Gorry and Scott Morton framework it is not based on the premise that there are generic types of decisions but rather it allows for the uniqueness of each organization.

An advantage of the framework is that it can be used to assess the extent to which DSS staff are being used to address the more difficult problems within an organization, and allows the DSS staff to map the progression they are making towards helping management to address the more difficult problems in their organization.

REFERENCES

Antill, L. (1985) Selection of a research method. In G. Fitzgerald, E. Mumford, R. Hirschheim and A.T. Wood Harper (eds), *Research Methods in Information Systems,* Elsevier Science Publishers, North-Holland, pp. 203-205.

Gorry, A. and Morton, S. (1971) A framework for management information systems. *Sloan Management Review*, 13(1): 55-70, Fall.

Ginzberg, M. and Stohr, E. A. (1982) Decision support systems: issues and perspectives. In decision support systems, North-Holland Publishing Company.

Hogue, J. T., (1982) A field study of the role of management in DSS. Unpublished PhD dissertation, University of Georgia, Athens.

Kirs, P. J. et al. (1989) An experimental validation of the Gorry and Scott Morton framework. *MIS Quarterly,* 13(2): 183-197. June.

Keen, P. (1987) MIS research: current states, trends and needs. In Richard A. Buckingham et al. (eds), *Information Systems Education: Recommendations and Implementation*, Cambridge University Press, pp 1- 13.

Moore, J. H. and Chang, M. (1983) Meta-design considerations. In J. L. Bennett (ed.), *Building Decision Support Systems*, Addison-Wesley, pp. 173-204

Mintzberg, H., (1982) Commentary on the Huber, Kunseuther and Schoemaker, and Chestnut and Jacoby papers. In Ungson and Braunstein, *Decision Making: An interdisciplinary Inquiry*, Kent Publishers. pp. 280-287,

Quillard, J. et al. (1983) A study of the corporate use of computers. Technical Report, MIT Centre for Information Systems Research. CISR Working Paper Number 109.

Simon, H. (1947) *Administrative Behaviour.* Macmillan, New York.

Simon, H. (1967) Information can be managed. *Think,* 33(3): 9-12.

Srinivasan, V. and Yong, K. (1986) Decision support for integrated cash management. *Decision Support Systems,* (2): 347-363.

Sprague, R. (1980) A framework for the development of decision support systems. *MIS Quarterly,* 4(4): 1-26.

15 CoverStory — automated news finding in marketing[*]

J. Schmitz[1], G. Armstrong[2] and J. Little[3]
1 Information Resources, Waltham, Massachusetts
2 Ocean Spray Cranberries, Lakeville-Middleboro, Massachusetts
3 Massachusetts Institute of Technology, Cambridge, Massachusetts

15.1 INTRODUCTION

Machine-readable bar codes on products in supermarkets have changed forever the way the packaged-goods industry tracks its sales and understands how its markets work. Although the codes were originally introduced and justified to save labour at check-out, the spin-off data produced by them provides marvellous opportunities for retailers and manufacturers to measure the effectiveness of marketing programmes and to create greater efficiencies in their merchandising and promotion. Ocean Spray Cranberries, Inc. has responded to these opportunities with an innovative decision support system designed to serve marketing and sales management.

15.1.1 Ocean Spray

Ocean Spray Cranberries, Inc. is a grower-owned agricultural cooperative headquartered in Lakeville-Middleboro, Massachusetts with about 900 members. It produces and distributes a line of high-quality juices and juice drinks with heavy emphasis on cranberry drinks but also with strong lines in grapefruit and tropical drinks. The company also has a significant business in cranberry sauces and fresh cranberries. About 80% of Ocean Spray products sell through supermarkets and other retail stores with lesser amounts flowing through food service and ingredient product channels. Ocean Spray is a Fortune 500 company with sales approaching $1 billion per year.

Until the mid-1980s, Ocean Spray, like most grocery manufacturers, tracked the sales and share of its products with syndicated warehouse withdrawal data and retail store data provided by such companies as SAMI and A. C. Nielsen. This data supplemented the company's own shipments data by providing information on competitive products and the total market.

---

[*]Reprinted from *Interface*

15.1.5 Ocean Spray's InfoScan database

Ocean Spray's syndicated database for juices is impressive, almost imposing, considering the change from the past and the level of human resources put against it. It contains about 400 million numbers covering up to 100 data measures, 10,000 products, 125 weeks and 50 geographic markets. It grows by 10 million new numbers every four weeks. Finding the important news amid this detail and getting it to the right people in a timely fashion is a big task for only one department.

15.1.6 Hardware and software

The DSS architecture puts the database and CPU-intensive processing on an IBM 9370 mainframe with ten gigabytes of disk storage and puts user-interface tasks on eleven 386-level workstations located in the marketing and sales areas. The basic DSS software is IRI's DataServer, which manages data and mainframe computation in the fourth-generation language EXPRESS and the user interface in pcEXPRESS. This provides menu-driven access to a family of flexible, preprogrammed reports available on the workstations.

Unlike some other solutions used by packaged-goods manufacturers, this architecture provides easy access to mainframe computing power from the workstations as is needed, for example, to run applications like the CoverStory software.

15.2   BASIC RETRIEVAL AND REPORTING

The basic retrieval, reporting and analytic capabilities of Ocean Spray's DSS are extensive. Any particular fact from the database can be pulled out in a few steps with the help of pull-down menus and pick lists. Much of the use comes from standard reports: a company top-line report, and four business area reports (cranberry drinks, grapefruit, aseptic packages and tropical drinks) showing status and trends including changes in share in aggregate and in detail, and changes in merchandising and distribution against a year ago or against four weeks ago. Derived measures such as BDI (brand development indices) and CDI (category development indices) are available. Product managers can get a quick update of what is going on with their products. Standardized graphs can be called up, and it is easy to construct new ones. Similarly, users can readily construct measures that are ratios, differences and other combinations of ones already in the database.

for each of the marketing factors such as distribution, price, displays, featuring and price cuts. These factor weights are intended, informally speaking, to make different marketing changes have the same score if their impact on sales is the same. We initialize factor weights based on analysis done outside of CoverStory based on logit models of the type described in Guadagni and Little (1983). Market weight is a term that makes it more likely that an event in a large market will be mentioned than an event in a small market. We originally used market size but found that this was too strong. Only events from New York, Chicago and Los Angeles would be mentioned, and so we have softened the impact of market size. One approach that has proven effective is to use the square root of market size as the market weight.

In all, this scoring method yields a ranked list of causal market changes where such a change can be described in terms of

- What happened? (for example, price went up by 20 percent);
- Where did it happen? (for example, in the southern region);
- What product did it happen to? (for example, the 32-ounce bottle).

The events that CoverStory describes are the ones that rank highest using this scoring mechanism.

15.3.7 Presenting the results

We have experimented with several methods for presenting these results. Our present style is to produce an English-language report in distribution-quality format. This has been an important piece of the overall effort and has had a dramatic effect on the acceptability of CoverStory reports to end-users. The language generation is straightforward; it is based on sentence templates (Barr and Feigenbaum 1981). We have considered but not yet implemented context and memory (Schank and Riesbeck 1981) in our text generation. The use of some randomization of detailed wording through the use of a thesaurus keeps the CoverStory memo from sounding too mechanical. The memo is relatively short and structured so this simple language generation has not been a limitation on CoverStory. The CoverStory results are published through a high-quality desk-top publishing package or a word-processor with desk-top publishing capabilities. Variation in typeface, use of graphic boxes and sidebars are all intended to give the memo visual appeal and highlight the marketing facts it contains.

CoverStory is very much a decision support system rather than a decision-making system. The user can adjust all major system parameters, such as who competes with whom, what weights to use for the marketing factors, and how much information is to be reported. The final memo is published through a standard word-processing package so it can be edited by the user, although this seldom happens. Because the memo is automated and easily set up (and then left alone) to meet the needs of specific managers, the appropriate 'news' can be distributed quickly throughout the organizations when new data arrives.

An excerpt from a CoverStory memorandum (page 238) illustrates the output. In this coded example, we present highlights about a brand called Sizzle in the United States. The recipient for this memorandum is the Sizzle brand manager and the brand management team. The series of decompositions in this report is:

- Break down total Sizzle volume into sales by size groups;
- Look at Sizzle's major competitors;
- Look at submarkets of the US − cities in this database;
- Look at competitive activity in these submarkets.

The analysis is based on share change. A sample of a causal change shown by CoverStory is the increase of display activity to support 64-ounce bottles of Sizzle.

15.4   BENEFITS

Ocean Spray's DSS design strategy has successfully solved several problems. The decision to put users in charge of their own basic retrieval and analysis has generally worked well and, where it has run into problems, the DSS organization has responded by providing increasingly customized tools. The DataServer interface has been easy to learn. Usage on the 386-level workstations located in the marketing area is many hours per week and rising.

The strategy casts the DSS organization in the role of acquiring and building tools to make the users more effective. Consultation with users has led to a set of hard-copy reports that are circulated regularly to marketing, sales and top management and to customized reports that can be called up on-line and printed locally on laser printers, if needed.

CoverStory is a particularly desirable development because, with very little effort, it provides users with top line summaries and analyses across a wide variety of situations. Previously this required time-consuming intervention by a skilled analyst. Furthermore, the technology is an extensible platform on which to build increasingly sophisticated decentralized analysis for the user community.

The information coming out of Ocean Spray's marketing DSS is used every day in planning, fire-fighting and updating people's mental models of what is going on in the company's markets. Typical applications include such actions as taking a price increase and monitoring its effect; discovering sales softness in a particular market, diagnosing its causes and applying remedies; and following a new product introduction to alert the sales department in case of weak results in certain markets compared to others. The DSS is totally integrated into business operations, and it no longer seems possible to consider life without it.

Perhaps the easiest way to express the success of the system is that, with the help of marketing science and expert systems technology, the DSS has made it possible for a single marketing professional to manage the process of alerting all Ocean Spray marketing and sales managers to key problems and opportunities and to provide them with daily problem-solving information and guidance. This is being done across four business units handling scores of company products in dozens of markets representing hundreds of millions of dollars of sales.

REFERENCES

Barr, A. and Feigenbaum, E. A. (eds) (1981) *Handbook of Artificial Intelligence,* William Kaufman Inc., Los Altos, California.

Guadagni, P. M. and Little, J. D. C. (1983) A logit model of brand choice calibrated on scanner data, *Marketing Science,* Vol. 2, No. 3 (Summer), pp. 203-238.

Little, J. D. C., (1979) Decision support systems for marketing managers, *Journal of Marketing,* Vol. 43, No. 3 (Summer), pp. 9-26.

Little, J. D. C., (1988) CoverStory: an expert system to find the news in scanner data, Working paper, Sloan School of Management, MIT (September).

McCann, J. M. (1986) *The Marketing Workbench,* Dow Jones-Irwin, Homewood, Illinois.

Schank, R. C. and Riesbeck, C. K. (eds) (1981) *Inside Computer Understanding,* Lawrence Erlbaum Associates, Hillsdale, New Jersey.

Stoyiannidis, D. (1987) A marketing research expert system, Sloan School Master's Thesis, MIT, Cambridge, Massachusetts (June).

To: **Sizzle Brand Manager**
From: CoverStory
Date: 10/29/90
Subject: **Sizzle Brand Summary for Twelve Weeks Ending October 7, 1990**

Sizzle's share of type in Total United States was 8.3 in the C&B Juice/Drink category for the twelve weeks ending 10/7/89. This is an increase of 0.2 points from a year earlier but down .3 from last period. This reflects volume sales of 8.2 million gallons. Category volume (currently 99.9 million gallons) declined 1.3% from a year earlier.

Sizzle's share of type is 8.3 - up 0.2 from the same period last year.

Display activity and unsupported price cuts rose over the past year - unsupported price cuts from 38 points to 46. Featuring and price remained at about the same level as a year earlier.

Components of Sizzle Share

Among components of Sizzle, the principal gainer is:

> Sizzle 64oz: up 0.5 points from last year to 3.7

and losers:

> Sizzle 48oz -0.2 to 1.9
>
> Sizzle 32oz -0.1 to 0.7

Sizzle 64oz's share of type increase is partly due to 11.3 pts rise in % ACV with Display vs yr ago.

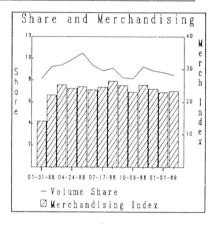

Share and Merchandising

— Volume Share
☑ Merchandising Index

Competitor Summary

Among Sizzle's major competitors, the principal gainers are:

> Shakey: up 2.5 points from last year to 32.6
>
> Private Label +.5 to 19.9 (but down .3 since last period)

and loser

> Generic Seltzer -.7 to 3.5

Shakey's share of type increase is associated with 71.7 pts of ACV rise in ACV Wtd Dist versus a year ago.

Market Highlights

Sizzle showed significant gains relative to a year ago in:

16 Management information Atlas Copco AB

T. Gannholm
Consultant in Administrative Development/Management Control,
Stockholm, Sweden

Do you have the best available information for your decisions? Is it enough to have a 'feeling' how business is progressing?

With today's potential to obtain information there is a great deal of information available. Therefore it often may be necessary to put the question: 'Which information is important, and is it reliable?'

As these techniques are improved, our demands are set higher still. It is now easier to select and move information between different management tools in order to analyse it and one has a better chance to obtain better control over the business.

What we call EIS (Executive Information Systems), are becoming more frequent but are in no way self-propelling. Does management appreciate the need for maintenance of such systems, as well as how the databases must be constructed in order to benefit the users of information in the best possible way?

A major problem is how to set the level of ambition. It must be considered as wishful thinking to believe that if you have lots of information in databases together with an EIS, it is only necessary for the boss to press a button and immediately the answer is there. Unfortunately some of the presentations of EIS give that impression.

In order to obtain any useful benefit from a certain amount of information it is absolutely necessary to understand what it represents. In my opinion it is important to know what is what. We must therefore differentiate between the management database and the management tools that are used in the EIS.

The management database must be neutral in the sense that it must be possible to identify each particular piece of information in it. Furthermore one must be able to deduce the information back to the source. Consequently it is not appropriate to manipulate information between various systems (databases) without clearly indicating what has been done.

When information has been transferred into the management database it must be readily accessible and from there be possible to extract and analyse with various management tools. For such a database a *sponsor* is required, i.e. somebody must have full responsibility for the quality of the data in the database as well as assisting the user when required. This might include the task to extract limited information from the database for certain managers which they can further analyse. The question of having a responsible person is valid for all databases and systems. In order to guarantee the quality of the information in a company, every subsystem needs to have somebody especially appointed to be responsible for a particular database. Otherwise the risk is great that when something is wrongly recorded or reported nobody will notice it.

The information in the management database must be readily available for the user with the management tool or combination of tools he or she prefers to use, and it must be possible to easily transfer the information between various management tools independently of which operating system the user prefers to use on his desk computer. From this it follows that an EIS cannot be a closed shop where suppliers of systems can prevent management tools other than their own to access the information.

The above-mentioned way of just pressing a button in order to obtain the answer is that such reports instead of only being produced on hard copy now are also available on the computer screen. No doubt this is a quicker way of distribution but in most cases the reports still have to be specified or prepared before being released. It is important that such reports are kept to a minimum and should preferably give only key figures. What many people understand by EIS is, however, merely the possibility to obtain such standard reports and diagrams. The above could be a very expensive way to obtain these reports and, if there is not a full understanding of the information and its uses, the EIS could cost an enormous amount of money in comparison with what it will be used for.

From my experience the above is not at all clear. The internal communication within a company, i.e. how a certain piece of information should be interpreted as well as who should have access to it, varies very much. I have several years of experience in how to view a company's relations between various quantities of information as well as managing projects aimed at executing such productivityi-mproving measures. Notice that managers from different departments often do not communicate on the same level, especially when money is involved. In those instances it is necessary to sit down with those managers and calibrate their communication. Again I must stress that the computer does not solve any problem, it only works as a very efficient tool in the hands of the user.

I strongly believe that the most important part of an EIS is the database from which it is simple and speedy to select and extract information for further analysis normally in the finance department. The standard reports are only a by-product which of course should be distributed through the computer network. Deeper analysis might be requested by top management but very seldom performed by them personally.

16.1 CHARACTERISTICS AND REQUIREMENTS OF AN ADVANCED EXECUTIVE INFORMATION SYSTEM

- Fresh data should be readily available.
- It must be possible to organize the information and extract essentials.
- Readable and relevant reports should be easy to produce.
- Data must be readily transferable between different applications and user.
- There should be a password access system to protect sensitive data.
- All this must be possible without first having to gain specialized computer knowledge.

It also needs to be recognized that many managers neither have the time, not should educate themselves, to become computer experts. I have particular difficulty in understanding those managers who make it difficult in spending a lot of time learning the operating system of a personal computer when their only objective is, in a serious way, to use the computer as a management tool and are not especially interested in deeper knowledge of computer techniques.

They could avoid all this extra work and concentrate on the tool if they instead use a personal computer in such a way that the user only has to switch on the computer and never sees the operating system. This latter built-in user-friendly way of working shows much higher productivity for managers than if they try to use a personal computer where they have to learn the operating system and then between each sporadic use of the computer have forgotten part of what they are supposed to do.

16.2 SIMPLE INFORMATION SYSTEMS COMPLYING WITH THE ABOVE ARE USED TODAY

At group management at Atlas Copco AB the controllers department and one executive vice-president is using such a system (BusinessPilot) for financial Group Information from subsidiaries around the world. This system has been developed in the powerful relational database, 4th DIMENSION, which is run on user-friendly Macintosh personal computers. 4th DIMENSION is in this case both a database and a tool. However, the database could have been in one of many environments without the user ever noticing it.

Without any computer knowledge, managers may select, sort and analyse the information required as well as obtaining standard reports on their screen and/or obtaining a hard copy.

All financial information which leaves an Atlas Copco subsidiary has a preset layout, common for the group. This information (balance sheets, profit and loss reports, sales statistics etc.) is created in the subsidiary and converted into a text file, either through the tailormade standard package limited to certain types of computers, or directly from an electronic spreadsheet such as EXCEL, where, with the help of a simple formula, the local report is converted into the standard layout for transmission via the network (MEMO) to the central database in the IBM mainframe in Nacka, Sweden. This information then has to be analysed by management in order to be of any use.

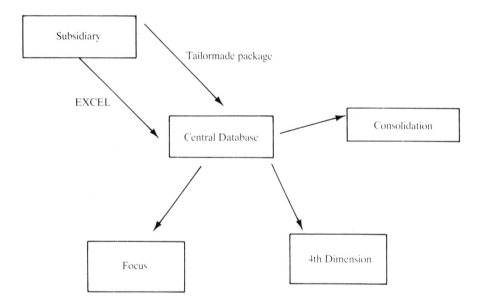

This is presently done in two ways:

1. For the computer expert, the most popular media is perhaps with the computer language called FOCUS, which, however, is too difficult for normal users to learn and makes them frustrated.

2. The other way is to go the user-friendly way, as at Atlas Copco group headquarters. Here, a copy of the central database is available on the

local network that connects the Macintoshes at group headquarters. The local network could very well be directly connected to the database in the IBM mainframe. This is, however, a matter of cost. It is much cheaper to have a copy of the database in the local network than always access the mainframe. Further, it may be faster as the load is lower.

Every person connected to the network and who has an authorized password has access to the information he needs and, in a very easy way, is able to select relevant details, sort them, analyse them or if required transfer them to the spreadsheet EXCEL for further analysis, or/and, if necessary, create his own reports on the printer.

16.2.1 At subsidiary level the scenario could be the following

The financial information for a couple of periods (years) is readily available in the BusinessPilot system. If you are a group with your own subsidiaries, the information from these companies will also be there. In addition to this information, you will have the sales statistics at the detail level required. The invoice lines are imported into your BusinessPilot system, probably every morning depending on how you work, and all marketing statistics will then be easily analysed by all marketing-responsible personnel at customer-level, article-level, PGC-level (product group) etc. This also goes for other types of statistics, hire fleets etc.

If, however, in every instant you need to have the latest transactions in your statistics, the 4th DIMENSION is able to reach your mainframe database (this can be done with a standardized programming language like DAL (formerly called CL/1) or APPC (Advanced Program to Program Communication). The communiction between the Macintosh and the IBM mainframe, the AS400 or the VAX computer is excellent. It is interesting to note that Apple as the first non-IBM company has got approval from IBM to use APPC to work against IBM's computers. The difference between DAL and APPC is that, with DAL, the job is done in the Macintosh while the mainframe functions as a database organizer; with APPC the work is divided between the two computers that communicate.

In order to download the data you want to analyse in your BusinessPilot system from your mainframe computer you will need an IRMA card, network control unit like Netway 1000 or similar connection, depending on the type of mainframe.

The method described is probably the easiest and most cost-effective way of giving managers the information they need. As mentioned earlier it is not the quantity of information that counts but the quality of information in combination with an intelligent selection of information. According to productivity analysis by reputed firms like the Gartner group and Peat Marwick, the user-friendly Macintosh has a productivity advantage of 25% or more over other PC-environments. In Sweden, Volvo Bussar AB, Molnlycke AB, ABB Corporate Research, Tetrapak and Swedish Televerket all use Macintosh around their IBM mainframes with similar or higher productivity gains as mentioned in the reports above.

Further, in order to use this equipment, you don't need to learn any complicated commands, as you have to do in other personal computer systems.

16.3 AN INTERESTING PARALLEL TO THE ABOVE WAY OF THINKING IS THE FOLLOWING

I have my roots very deep in the Baltic island of Gotland. Antiquarian finds including precious metals and coins found in the soil of Gotland are tremendous. There are plenty of books written about Gotland, which can be compared to databases for various departments in a company. Still you very often hear the question 'Why do we know so little about the history of the people of Gotland?' The way of working in a company is a way of across-the-borders science. As the above question has bothered me for a long time, I sat down and started analysing the source documents (some metres of bookshelves) from historians, archaeologists, linguists, philologists, astronomers etc. concerning Gotland. I could here use a very similar approach to what I have described above when I analyse a company.

Of course I had to be very observant on the quality of the information and when necessary go back to the primary source of information.

The computer was of tremendous help to me but could naturally only function as a tool. All the conclusions I had to do myself as I have to do in a company. The result was overwhelming and I could extract information previously unknown.

By working in this manner I discovered that the island was already thebusiness centre in the Baltic during the Bronze Age and the Gotlandic people had lots of contacts and business with the Romans. This position the people of Gotland kept until the fourteeth century.

With advanced tools connected to my Macintosh the book *Butarnas Historia* was, in a short time, wholly produced on my computer and 224 pages of film were presented to the printers in order to print the book.

The transferability of information as well as pictures was very simple in this environment and the result could, without too much trouble, be presented in a very professional way.

To conclude, the principles of working with information is very similar: either you work with business information in a company or you work with scientific matters.

16.4 COMPUTERS HAVE CHANGED THE WAY OF ADMINISTRATIVE ROUTINES IN A COMPANY

When the routines were manual each function controlled its own activities but only for its limited purposes. From management's point of view it was difficult to get a full picture over the operations. The sales department for instance recorded the sales statistics. The supply department kept the stock records and at the end of each year these were added up and valued and the difference between purchases and material in stock was accepted as cost of goods sold.

The accounts department recorded and kept all money transactions within the financial department. For official purposes these were of course the only valid records.

All other records were considered statistics only and nobody bothered whether the statistical information agreed with that in the financial ledger. Information about the company's result was merely produced for legal purposes. Further it was compiled very late and was only a statement of how the company managed the previous year.

In order to get a better control of the company and also to some degree use it as a management tool the general ledger was organized in classes. This was not a bad system although cumbersome in a manual environment. It was, however, difficult to know whether a product made a profit or not.

When administrative systems are being computerized or transferred to a new computer system, the normal procedure has been to transfer the present routines to the new system. At best, smaller 'improvements are undertaken resulting in systems which are too difficult and hinder rather than simplify access to information. Routines might not be improved or abolished as it is not sure that analyses to establish its feasibility are undertaken. When administrative routines are allowed to develop by themselves they tend to be uneven and complicated. The cost for electronic processing of the information will therefore be unnecessarily expensive.

Furthermore, administrative departments tend to be overstaffed resulting in bureaucracy. The human nature tries to justify a position and make sure that there is enough work merely by creating work which at an objective study is not necessary for the operation. There are very few people who can see the whole chain of events in the administrative routines from the sales tender over the production and invoicing to the final balance sheet.

This is necessary in order to simplify and shorten the routines and controls of the business. With a well thought-out computer system it does not need to be too complicated to have full control over this matter.

My philosophy is that in a group of companies with similar business it is possible to have standard administrative packages. Too often I hear the computer people, when installing a new system, ask: 'What are the changes needed in order to adapt this package to your local requirements?' My attitude is that this question should not be allowed. Instead the users must be asked: 'How can you simplify your routines in order to make best use of this package?'

Information from administrative systems is primarily intended for decision making and secondarily for legal requirements. Therefore no information should be produced that does not fulfil the above requirements.

From the user's point of view a system must be as simple as possible. The data should be available on a database and easily transferable and accessible for analysing on the desk computer of the person concerned.

Here comes the important task to streamline and simplify the routines before starting the new system. Sometimes it might be necessary to drastically change the routines in order to make them more functional and obtain a more logical flow of information.

We must not fall into the old trap where the user demands to have the system changed in order to suit his or her routines. The system is the tool with which we work, and when the old routine is not working on the new system we must see how the routine can be changed and simplified in order to have it fit into the company's total flow of information.

Too much effort and money are wasted on cumbersome administrative systems. These have come about by people having formed the systems to suit their immediate needs. This was probably correct at the time of introduction but circumstances and techniques change very rapidly. Therefore it is important to go through the routines from time to time and make sure that not more is done than is required in order to run the operation in an efficient way.